Truth

Central Problems of Philosophy

Series Editor: John Shand

This series of books presents concise, clear, and rigorous analyses of the core problems that preoccupy philosophers across all approaches to the discipline. Each book encapsulates the essential arguments and debates, providing an authoritative guide to the subject while also introducing original perspectives. This series of books by an international team of authors aims to cover those fundamental topics that, taken together, constitute the full breadth of philosophy.

Published titles

Free Will
Graham McFee

Knowledge
Michael Welbourne

Relativism
Paul O'Grady

Truth
Pascal Engel

Universals
J. P. Moreland

Forthcoming titles

Action
Rowland Stout

Analysis
Michael Beaney

Artificial Intelligence
Matthew Elton & Michael Wheeler

Causation and Explanation
Stathis Psillos

Meaning
David Cooper

Mind and Body
Robert Kirk

Modality
Joseph Melia

Ontology
Dale Jacquette

Paradox
Doris Olin

Perception
Barry Maund

Rights
Jonathan Gorman

Scepticism
Neil Gascoigne

Self
Stephen Burwood

Value
Chris Cherry

Truth

Pascal Engel

First published in 2002 by Acumen

Acumen Publishing Limited
15a Lewins Yard
East Street
Chesham
Bucks HP5 1HQ
www.acumenpublishing.co.uk

ISBN: 1-902683-57-9 (hardcover)
ISBN: 1-902683-58-7 (paperback)

British Library Cataloguing-in-Publication Data
A catalogue record for this book is available from
the British Library.

Designed and typeset by Kate Williams, Abergavenny.
Printed and bound by Biddles Ltd., Guildford and King's Lynn.

Contents

Preface

Philosophical work on truth has been quite abundant during recent decades. This book is an introduction to this work, but one that does not go into the wealth of logical detail that has often characterized a number of treatments of these issues. Moreover, as the topic touches most other subjects within the broad areas of philosophical logic, semantics and epistemology – such as the nature of the bearers of truth and falsity, quantification, vagueness, reference, conditionals, modal and intuitionist logics, logical paradoxes, and the definitions of knowledge and justification – the reader will not find here the technicalities that provide both the difficulty and the charm of a large battle fought on so many fronts. Instead I have preferred to focus on the overall map of the battle, and to indicate the significance of the various theories for the rest of philosophy. This is why the book is centrally concerned with one of the most discussed topics in the recent philosophical literature, the "deflationist" or "minimalist" theories of truth. They are attractive because they promise to solve or to dissolve some of the main problems of philosophy – such as the debates between realism and anti-realism – by making truth a relatively simple thing. But their apparent modesty hides in fact quite ambitious and complex implications, which I have tried to describe, and which, it seems to me, far from showing that the problem of the nature of truth can be put to one side and make us free to deal with other questions, obliges us to think more about why truth matters.

During recent years I have been much helped by exchanges on these issues with Paul Boghossian, Donald Davidson, Paul Horwich,

Wolfgang Künne, Kevin Mulligan, Alberto Voltolini, Marco Santambrogio and Paolo Leonardi, especially when the last two organized a summer school in 1999 on this very topic and another one on normativity in 2000. My debt towards the writings of Crispin Wright, even when I disagree with him, should be obvious. I thank Bob Almeder and Susan Haack for their helpful remarks on some parts of the manuscript, David Armstrong and David Wiggins for letting me see some of their unpublished writings, and Stelios Virvidakis and Jérôme Dokic for their encouragement. I am most grateful to John Shand and Steven Gerrard for having proposed that I rethink these issues within this series, and to the lucid comments made by two anonymous referees, which I hope I have taken into account. Some years ago, in Bristol, I met Christopher Williams, who offered me a copy of his *What is Truth?* When I came to understand the value of his pioneering contribution, it was too late to discuss it with him. I dedicate this book to his memory.

Introduction: Truth lost?

Truth is a central philosophical notion, perhaps *the* central one. Many other important philosophical notions depend upon it or are closely tied to it: thought; belief (to believe something is to believe that it is *true*); knowledge (if one knows a proposition, then it is *true*); reality (reality is what our *true* statements, beliefs and theories are about); existence or being (can we talk *truly* about nonexistents?); fact (facts are what make our statements *true*); possibility and necessity (can one say something *true* about what is merely possible? Are there propositions which can be *true* in all possible worlds?); and many other kindred notions such as proposition, sentence, statement, assertion, entailment, and so on. It is also central because it seems to be what theoretical life is about, or what it aims at. Science is said to be a search for truth; perhaps this also applies to philosophy and other disciplines. Practical life, by contrast, is said to be the search for the good, or the just, and does not result in things that are true or false; but many philosophers claim that the good or the just are objects of knowledge, and in so far as knowledge involves truth, this notion is relevant in the practical realm as well. Even if ethics is not to be understood as a matter of knowledge of certain truths (but, say, as a matter of expression and regulation of feelings), it is important to understand the nature of truth in order to see the contrast. This applies to aesthetics too: is judging that something is beautiful a matter of knowing certain truths? And if not, what is the difference between aesthetic discourse and truth-seeking discourse? It is similar for evaluating the differences between metaphorical and literal discourse, poetry and prose, rhetoric and science, fiction and non-fiction, historiography and narrative, and so on. So to understand what truth is, what role this fundamental notion plays in our ordinary as well as in our more sophisticated conceptual schemes, seems to be a major philosophical task.

Yet much of contemporary thinking is very suspicious of talk in terms of truth. Pilate is known for having jested, "What is truth?" (John 18: 38), and he seems to have many disciples today. Phrases such as "the disinterested search for truth" arouse mockery. Even scientists are cautious about saying that they produce true theories of the world: they prefer to talk of "models". Only leaders of sects or religious people are not afraid of such talk. Philosophers themselves, at least from Nietzsche onward, have made us wary of it. It has a smell of scientism, or of positivism, and in any case of utter naivety. For a number of contemporary thinkers truth is a sort of "relic of a bygone age", as Russell (1912) famously said about the notion of cause in today's physics. Have not writers such as Foucault shown us that behind such talk, in science as well as in philosophy and religion, there lies a will to power, an ideological bias that hides other aims that are all but disinterested? A pervasive feature of contemporary postmodernism is that the will for truth is deeply suspect, and that the traditional idea that there could be one true story about the world is not only wrong but obnoxious. One dominant trend in the field known as "science studies" claims that "laboratory life" is not guided by the ideals of objectivity and truth, which are classically considered to be the aims of scientific enquiry, but by a certain social organization of scientific work, and by patterns of power relationships. Perhaps, it is suggested, there is no such thing as Truth, but there are many truths, truth for X or truth for Y, or truth in this context and truth in that context, and hence no truth in itself. Relativism, or even nihilism, about truth thus seem to be the only alternatives. Any discourse that would promote itself as having the right to say *the* truth is suspect, and it is just another narrative, equally "justified", but equally arbitrary. Truth, in such views, is merely an effect, a projection of our discourses onto a fictional "reality in itself". The question, as Humpty Dumpty would say, is which is to be master.

Relativists and sceptics about truth, however, are well aware that their rejection of this notion as illusory does little to prevent it from being used in ordinary life and in common-sense talk. However disenchanted we can be with Truth with a capital T, we keep on talking about true and false opinions, or true or false theories, and it is important for us to avoid error, to avoid cheats and to denounce lying. The sceptics do not deny that there exists, in each field of enquiry, and in particular in science, more or less objective criteria for sorting out the true from the false. And even those sophisticated Nietzschean philosophers who have accused Logos or Rationality of serving tyrannical ends are reluctant to get rid of truth talk completely when, for instance, they engage in political battles where it is important to keep track of liars and to promote truth and justice. Sceptics about truth are here in the same predicament as ordinary sceptics about knowledge of the external world: just as the latter can't help acting and thinking in a world that they have to take, in one way or another, as *real*, the former cannot deny that there are things that we assert, that there are beliefs that we have, and that our ordinary talk is such that we assess them as *true* or not. When such sceptics want to know whether the piece of furniture that they bought from an antique shop is authentic, they seem to be just like everyone else, caring about what is *true*. The proper line to take, for such sceptics, is not to deny that we have any *use* of the concept of truth in our common practices, or that the word "true" does not have any sense. What they have to say, rather, is that behind such talk there is no real common feature, or common essence, which would underlie its uses. On such a view, the word "true" indeed has a certain meaning, but this meaning just amounts to the fact that we use it as term of praise or approval for some of our assertions or some of our theories, when we want to promote them against others. As Richard Rorty, one of the main defenders of such a "postmetaphysical" conception of truth puts it, truth is but a "compliment" that we pay to our favourite assertions, or a little pat on the back that we give them. On this view, "true" serves to express the fact that *we* value some of our statements, but it is not in itself a value or a property that would lie behind our various attitudes of approval, or our practices of sorting out the views that we like by calling them "true", from those that we don't like by calling them "false". Apart from that, there is not much more to say, and the various philosophical attempts to define truth as a more profound and deep metaphysical notion are misguided.

A number of contemporary philosophers, however, resist such disenchanted conceptions of truth. They are faithful to the traditional view according to which there are at least some regions of discourse, in particular in science, which are truth-apt, that is, susceptible to be assessed for truth and falsity. They agree that the claim that we can describe or "mirror" an independent reality is not easy to defend without all sorts of qualifications. But they still agree that truth is a least a regulative ideal, and that philosophy can be regarded as a theoretical attitude, which can produce arguments and evaluate them, as well as it can promote certain claims which can be confronted with "facts", however difficult it is to spell out. Analytic philosophy in the twentieth century, from its realist beginnings with Frege, Russell and Moore and its attempts during the logical positivist period to demarcate science from metaphysics, to its contemporary attraction for naturalism and scientific realism, illustrates the permanent appeal of talk in terms of truth and associated notions such as correspondence or verification. A major, and striking, difference between this tradition and the tradition known as "Continental philosophy" is that analytic philosophers have devoted a lot of effort to trying to account for the meaning of the simple word "true", and to discuss the various possible "theories of truth". They want to know what it means to say that our theories of the world are true, and whether they can be said to be so. They do not doubt that philosophers can play a major role in elucidating this. So they have investigated whether truth can be defined as correspondence between our statements and reality, or whether it could be defined as a form of coherence between our statements, or whether it can be defined, in the pragmatic sense, as a way of saying that a statement is useful or beneficial. In fact most of the history of twentieth-century analytic philosophy is a sort of battlefield opposing various "realist" and "anti-realist" conceptions of truth.

This is not say that one does not find, within the German idealist and postidealist tradition, various attempts to elucidate the notion of truth. Heidegger, for instance, devotes a great deal of effort to an examination of the Greek word *alètheia*, and to promoting a conception of truth as the revelation or disclosure of being (*Unverbogenheit*) or as the "event" (*Ereignis*) of being. Nietzsche is careful to analyse the ordinary meaning of the word "true", when he wants to claim that truth is only a "metaphor" and that we might be in love with it. But most of the time there is nothing comparable, within the contemporary Continental tradition, to the careful, minute, and scrupulous attempts of analytic philosophers to analyse our ordinary concept of truth, and to compare the various possible conceptions of it. In a sense, this is hardly surprising, for if one takes the philosophical belief in truth as a sort of illusion, the undermining or deconstruction of this illusion should play a larger role than the attempt to *construct* an acceptable meaning of this notion. For writers such as Foucault, for instance, it is much more important to try to show the *role* that the notion of truth plays in our discursive practices and in our social institutions (as a means of power and oppression) than to define it philosophically. In fact for him this social role or function is merely the definition of it, and truth has no hidden essence.

At this point, we might just shrug our shoulders: either you still believe in truth, or you don't, period. All the rest seems to be a dialogue of the deaf. This resembles, in many ways, the traditional conflict between sceptics and dogmatics, or the famous dialogue between Oscar Wilde and his judges, when they asked him whether he did not find his own writings "obscene" and he replied: "'Obscene' is not a word in my vocabulary." In the same manner some people seem to want to say: "'Truth' is not a word in my vocabulary."

There can, however, be some common ground of discussion between the truth-sceptics and the (let us call them) truth-nonsceptics. For in the course of their analyses of the ordinary notion of truth and in their examination of the various possible theories of truth, analytic philosophers themselves have encountered the idea which I have attributed to the truth-sceptics, that truth might not be a deep philosophical or metaphysical notion and that it might not denote any real property that our beliefs, propositions or theories might exemplify. On such a view, truth is not a weighty notion, but a very light or thin one, the meaning of which can be exhausted by such truisms as "A sentence is true if and only if things are the way it says they are", "To say that a sentence is true is just to assert it" or (for a given sentence "P") "'P' is true if and only if P." According to such views, which are called "deflationist" or "minimalist", the word "true" has this minimal sense, which is sufficient to account for most, or even all, our actual uses of it. There is not much more to say about it.

In fact, such minimalist conceptions of truth seem always to have been present in the philosophical tradition. They might underlie Aristotle's famous dictum that "To say of what is that it is, or of what is not that it is not, is true" (*Metaphysics* Γ, 7, 1011b, 26) or Descartes's claim that "truth is such a transcendentally clear notion that is cannot be further defined" (in a letter to Mersenne, Descartes 1964–76, II: 597). Frege himself, the founder of the analytic tradition, claimed that truth is an indefinable, absolutely primitive concept. Ramsey, Ayer and the logical positivists, and also Wittgenstein, held that the truism "'p' is true $= p$" exhausts the meaning of the word. Tarski has shown how one could devise definitions of truth for a given language by relying on such innocent equivalences as "'Snow is white' is true if and only if snow is white." And contemporary analytic philosophers, like Quine, have claimed that truth is just a device of "disquotation" of a sentence 'P' from a sentence "'P' is true", or like Davidson (1995), have denounced "the folly of trying to define truth". Thus the idea, to put it in Austin's terms, "that a theory of truth is but a collection of truisms" (Austin [1950] 1999: 152), has both a long ancestry in the history of philosophy, and a long descent in contemporary thinking. It seems to coincide, in many ways, with the truth-sceptics' intuition that truth talk is just a storm in a teacup. At this point, one may feel that some of the most sophisticated linguistic and logical analyses produced by present-day analytic philosophers come very close to the postmodernist idea that truth is just a word of approval, or a device of assertion of the claims that we like most, and in no way a genuine property. Thus the relativistic idea that we can say that some sentences are true because we assert them *from within* our discursive practices and not *from without* or from a transcendent "view from nowhere" is also present in analytic philosophy. For those who take analytic philosophy to be the heir of the classical conception of science, and philosophy as the "mirror" or representation of reality, this would come as a surprise. But for those, who, like Rorty (1982: 227), believe that we can imagine "a future in which the tiresome 'analytic–Continental split' is looked back upon as an unfortunate temporary breakdown of communication" between the two traditions, it will hardly be a surprise. So perhaps we have here, within the philosophy of truth, a common ground of discussion, a way to assess one of the major dividing lines between these traditions.

In this book, however, I shall not attempt to draw a systematic parallel between these two contemporary ways of theorizing (or antitheorizing) about truth.[1] My aim will be to present and discuss the main reflections about truth that analytic philosophers on the contemporary scene have elaborated. But I shall, at strategic moments, try to be attentive to some of the similarities adduced above between various sorts of deflationist moods within analytic philosophy and within Continental philosophy. Indeed, in many ways, one gets the feeling that when, on the one hand, Continental scepticism about truth reaches the more self-conscious stages of its reflections on the failure of truth, rationality and realism to be proper ideals of philosophic enquiry, it should avail itself of the resources of analytic thinking in this field, just to see where its arguments can lead; on the other hand, one also gets the feeling that when analytic philosophers are attracted by some antimetaphysical, anti-realist or minimalist conceptions of truth, they should take a pause and step backwards to think of how close they can come to some antitheoretical moods.

Nevertheless, there is a difference. A proper investigation into the concept of truth can lead us to resist the snares of relativism and scepticism, for at least three reasons. First, to say that truth could be a minimal concept, with no hidden essence, does not by itself imply that there is no *point* in using this concept, nor in talking about it, as some of the more radical sceptical thinkers seem to suggest. It is one thing to say that the concept of truth does not have the theoretical import that it seems to have, and another to say that we could get rid of it altogether. Think of the many important philosophical problems that would have no sense if the concept of truth were to vanish: the problem of realism in a number of areas and the problem of the reality of various entities (the nature of theories and of theoretical entities in science, the problem of abstract objects in mathematics, the nature and reality of values in ethics); the nature of meaning and semantics (which is often said to be a matter of truth conditions); a certain conception of logic (as dealing with a certain kind of truths), and so on. In contemporary thought, some philosophers, in particular Dummett, have proposed to consider the various disputes about realism as disputes about the nature of truth. They may be wrong but the suggestion that truth might disappear altogether from all these fields would make a lot of contemporary philosophy pointless. Second, the fact that truth is a "thin" concept does not imply that it does not carry with it certain constitutive commitments. In this sense, I want to argue, our ordinary notion of truth involves the idea that it is a norm of enquiry, and that the rejection of this normative character, wherever it comes from, threatens the very coherence of our theoretical endeavours. Now it might be objected that this threat is just the one that many sceptical or nihilistic contemporary conceptions let hang over our most serious rationalistic enterprises. To answer it, we do not only need to analyse our ordinary concept of truth, but also to get into an account of truth as a cognitive value. We need to see why it matters. This involves a comparison of this value with other values, in particular with ethical values. Indeed nihilism about truth is just a version of nihilism about values in general. So in the end, and in the third place, a proper philosophy of truth should lead to a proper appreciation of the respective roles of, and of the connections between, our theoretical and our practical values. This is, after all, what most of philosophy is about: a normative enquiry into the nature of our norms and values, and into the normativity and value of these very norms and values. So the philosophy of truth should not be foreign to it.

1 Classical theories of truth

1.1 A preliminary map

Before examining various classical philosophical conceptions of truth, let us try to characterize the main features of our naïve, commonsensical conception of it. We have a predicate, "true", in all languages[1] (*wahr, vrai, verum, alèthès, pravdy*, etc.), which we apply to all sorts of items – thoughts, beliefs, judgements, assertions, ideas, conceptions, views, theories, and so on – which seem to refer to the contents of our thoughts, which are abstract, or a least non-concrete, entities. We apply, however, this predicate also to concrete things, such as pictures, artefacts, pieces of currency, or even living animals. For instance we say that this is a *true* drawing by Poussin, that this is a *true* copy of a document, a *true* 50 euro banknote, a *true* piece of artillery or a *true* Irish setter. In such cases, the meaning of "true" seems to be the same as "authentic", "real", "faithful", "exact", or "conforming to" a model or a type. Sometimes too we employ "true" to characterize other sorts of properties, such as character traits, when for instance we talk of a *true* friend, meaning that the person is loyal or trustworthy.

All these meanings, however, seem to derive from two basic ones: "true" as a *property* of an item that makes it genuine, natural or real, as opposed to contrived, artificial or fictional; and "true" as a *relation* between some item *to which* the predicate is attributed, and some other item which *makes true* the first item. The former is what one calls, in the current philosophical vocabulary, the *truth-bearer*, and the latter what one calls the *truth-maker*. As we have just remarked, the truth-bearers are usually considered to be the content of information transmitted by various concrete entities, mental ("ideas") or physical (sentences, drawings on a piece of paper, patterns of symbols, sounds emitted), rather than the concrete entities themselves. It is uncontroversial that we often apply the predicate "true" to concrete physical items, such as sentences (sequences of sounds or symbols), but it seems clear that we attribute it to the content of the sentences, rather than to the physical entities of which they are made up. We say "This sentence is true", but we do not say "This sequence of sounds is true". Similarly when we say such things as "I wish my dreams came true", we refer to the content of our dreams, not to the psychological or physical events that appear in our brains. Finally, our ordinary notion of truth is such that when we say that a certain utterance or belief is true, we intend to say that it has a certain *further* characteristic than the mere fact that we *have* the belief or that the utterance has been performed. We use it to refer to an *objective* property that our beliefs, statements, and such like have, independently of us. In other words, the fact that we call something true or false seems to mark a real distinction between the things that have these properties and the things that don't. And we take it that this distinction is due to a property of our thoughts that they have in virtue of their relation to the real world.

This last feature also stands in contrast with another: our ordinary use of the word "true" is such that it simply marks the fact that we have endorsed an assertion or a statement. When someone says: "The volcano has erupted", and when someone else wants to agree, that person says: "It is true", meaning that he or she endorses the previous assertion. The two statements "The volcano has erupted" and "It is true that the volcano has erupted" do not exactly mean the same thing, for the latter contains the mark of approval, but in so far as what is said is concerned, they have the same cognitive content. In this sense the words "is true" do not designate a *further* characteristic from the fact that the sentence has this content: the predicate "is true" does not seem to be on a par with such properties as "is square" or "weighs 3 kilos". When we say that a thought is true, we do not seem to be attributing to it a genuine property. This potentially conflicts with the previous intuition that truth is an objective property of our thoughts.

So far this is not very philosophically controversial, although there is room to elaborate philosophical ideas from these simple observations. Philosophy starts when one remarks that it is not obvious that these features of our predicate "true" are features of a single, unified concept, and that it is not easy to define it. First, it is not evident what the bearers of truth are. A long philosophical tradition, going back to the Stoics and represented in contemporary philosophy by Frege and Carnap among others, claims that the truth-bearers are *propositions*, abstract entities expressed by linguistic sentences. Another tradition, going back to Descartes and classical empiricism, claims that the truth-bearers are *ideas*, beliefs, or mental representations (or sometimes "judgements", conceived as made up of ideas) that also carry a certain content, but that tends to be mental or psychological in nature. And some philosophers, from Ockham and Hobbes to Quine, have claimed that the bearers of truth are sentences or physical symbols, or at least entities locatable in space and time, like utterances.

Secondly, there is disagreement about what kind of property truth is. Let us leave aside for the moment the view that truth might not be a genuine property, and let us assume that it is a real characteristic. Some philosophers hold that truth is an *intrinsic* or *monadic* property of truth-bearers, one that they have absolutely and in virtue of nothing else, and not in relation to other things (for instance, *being happy* is a monadic property, whereas *being a brother* is a relational one). But the most common view is that truth is a *relational* property, that holds between truth-bearers and other entities. The most classical conception is that truth is a relation of *correspondence*, of adequacy or of fit, or perhaps *identity*, between the true items and something else, the truth-makers. Among such conceptions, there is disagreement about the nature of these truth-makers: some philosophers claim that they are entities of a different kind from truth-bearers – facts, states of affairs, or situations in the world; others do not make such fine distinctions and are happy to say that truth is correspondence with reality. Another relational conception is that truth is a relation between *the truth-bearers themselves*, that is, between propositions and other propositions, beliefs and other beliefs, sentences and other sentences, when they make some coherent whole. Such conceptions are called *coherence* conceptions of truth: according to such views, there is no need to appeal to truth-makers as some *further* entities and to a relation distinct from the one that holds between the truth-bearers. Or rather truth is not a property of truth-bearers, but of *sets* or *wholes* made up of them. Another view, *pragmatism*, is that truth relates to the *useful effects* of our conceptions. *Prima facie*, these conceptions are not equivalent or compatible: they involve quite distinct onto-logical commitments. At this point it seems that the philosophy of truth is part of metaphysics, and here as elsewhere there can be more or less economical, or more or less profligate, ontologies. Armed with such ontologies, the task is to account for the fact that truth is objective, and marks a genuine difference between truths and non-truths. To a large extent, this is what "theories of truth" are about. We can try to draw a preliminary map: see Figure 1.[2]

As we shall see, this figure does not exhaust the possible options. For instance option 2, that truth is not a genuine property, charac-terizes what we shall call *minimalist* theories, in contrast with

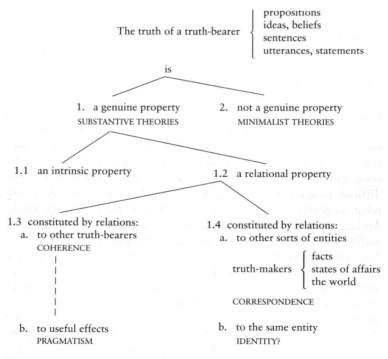

Figure 1

substantive ones. The full meaning of this contrast will only be appraised in Chapter 2. It is also important, when we say that the options indicated here characterize various "theories of truth", to be clear about what such a phrase means. It often refers to different kinds of questions, which can be easily conflated. One can ask: (a) "What is the *meaning* of our ordinary word 'true'"? and in general the answer will involve an account of the various central uses of this word in our language; (b) "What is our *concept* of truth?", and the answer will involve an account of the role played by this concept within our overall conceptual scheme, in relation to other concepts; (c) "What are the *criteria* of truth?", and the answer will involve an account of the means by which we recognize that something is true; (d) what truth *is*, and the answer will provide a *definition* of truth. Finally (e) there is also a sense of "theory of truth" and of "definition of truth" that occurs in the context of *axiomatic* theories of truth for a language, but we shall leave it aside for the moment and examine it in §2.3.

For the moment, let us restrict ourselves to questions (a)–(d). These correspond to separate enquiries, although they are obviously connected. One can give an account of the meaning of "true" without intending to say anything about what truth is, or by what epistemological criteria we identify it. And one can give these criteria without defining it. For instance, we can say that certainty is a criterion of truth without prejudging what truth is.[3] Similarly, it is one thing to elucidate what concept of truth we have, and another thing to say what truth is (compare: our concept of truth is the concept of a translucent liquid, but water is H_2O). But it seems difficult to say that our concept of truth has no relationship with what we mean by the word "true", nor with our criteria for truth. And in a sense, a definition of truth should tell us what this notion *really* means. Perhaps a more neutral term, such as "conception" or "account", would be more appropriate, but presumably a complete *theory* of truth, in the philosophical sense of this term, should try to answer all these questions, and to trace their connections. In general the classical theories of truth that we shall examine here all attempt to give *definitions* of truth, in the sense of explaining what the real nature or essence of this property is, even when they are prepared to recognize that truth might not be a property or a "thing" in the ordinary sense. The notion of definition, like that of analysis, admits a looser and a stricter sense: on the one hand an analysis or definition is an account of a concept and an elucidation of its connections with other concepts; on the other hand, it is a *real* definition, attempting to reduce an entity to other, simpler, ones, in the sense of a *reduction*. This means that we hope to provide something like necessary and sufficient conditions for a definition of truth in terms of another, more primitive, property. Now the notion of necessary and sufficient conditions is usually expressed by the logical connective "if and only if" (where the *if* conjunct is the sufficient condition, and the *only if* conjunct is the necessary condition"; abbreviated to "iff"). Hence our definitions can be framed under the following form of an equivalence (which we shall meet quite often):

(Def *T*)   X *is true iff* . . .

where "*X*" stands for some appropriate truth-bearer, and the blank on the right-hand side stands for some appropriate *definiens* or necessary and sufficient condition for X. The various "theories" of truth will aim first at filling this blank. Now if this necessary and sufficient condition stands for some real, explanatory property or set of properties, the theories in question will be called *substantive* or *robust* ones. Whether such theories make sense or not is one of the main questions that we have to address. The option that truth cannot be defined, and that the blank cannot be filled by a substantive explanation, does not figure explicitly in Figure 1, but it is an open one. As we shall see, it makes its appearance at every turn.

1.2 Correspondence

The most common definition of truth present in the philosophical tradition is the most intuitive one: truth is a relation of correspondence between the contents of our thoughts and reality, or between our judgements and facts:

(Correspondence)   X *is true iff* X *corresponds to the facts*

A correspondence conception of truth is often called a *realist* conception in the following sense: it says that our thoughts are true *in virtue* of something that is distinct from them, and independent from our thinking and knowing of them. In this sense, the truth of a statement is also supposed to *transcend* our possible knowledge of it, or its verification. In opposition, we may call *anti-realist* any conception of truth according to which truth does not transcend our cognitive powers, and is constrained by some epistemic condition. The use of the word "realism" at this stage of our enquiry is bound to be vague, for it will turn out that we shall be able to characterize a view as realist only when we are able to see whether, and if so in what sense, it involves a distinctive conception of truth. In this sense, any enquiry into the nature of truth will have to *construct* the various senses of "realism" at issue, and must not take it as given. Moreover, as we shall see, correspondence is not the only possible realist conception of truth. But we can, for the moment, use the general characterization just given. Correspondence theories are supposed to spell this out *in virtue of* a relation which is, to use the traditional scholastic phrase, a relation of "adequacy" of things to the intellect (*adaequatio rei et intellectus*).

It is often said that the first explicit formulation of this definition occurs in a famous passage in Aristotle's *Metaphysics* that I have already quoted: "To say of what is that it is not, and of what is not that it is, is false, while to say of what is that it is, or of what is not that it is not, is true" (*Metaphysics* Γ, 7, 1011b, 26). But this passage is far from clear. To take up our distinctions of the previous section, it is not obvious that Aristotle is here giving a definition of truth, rather than a characterization of the meaning of "true". In some passages, he explicitly talks of giving the meaning (*sèmainei*) of "true" with such equivalences (*Metaphysics* Δ 7, 1017a 31–5). In other passages, however, he is quite explicit about the idea of a relation between the thing, or rather the fact (*pragma*) and the truth of the proposition (*logos*), but he calls this relation a "cause" (*dia*): facts cause the truth of the proposition (*Categories*, 14b, 14, *Metaphysics* Θ 10, 1051 b 6).[4] And if it is a definition of truth in terms of a certain relation, Aristotle seems to say that is a relation of *identity* between what we say (or think) and reality, rather than a relation of *correspondence*. If to say what is *true* and to say what *is* (or what is false and what is not) is to say the same thing, truth and being are one and the same thing. But there is a difficulty here, for, as Aquinas says commenting upon this passage, if truth and being were the same thing, "it would be vain to talk about a true being, which is not the case; hence they are not identical". Truth, therefore, *adds* something to being, and this something is "a relationship of correspondence" or adequacy (*adaequatio*) between the thing and the intellect (*Questiones disputatae de veritate*: 1, 1–2, 8–9).[5] This definition is the one that has been adopted by the tradition. It can be found in Descartes, in Leibniz, in Hume, in Kant,[6] for instance. Most of the time, it seems to be taken up from the scholastic tradition without any real attempt to explain what it means, or to spell out the appropriate relation.[7]

If one jumps from the fourteenth century to the discussions that have shaped the contemporary versions of this view, it is interesting to note that Frege, one of the main founders of analytic philosophy, stumbles about the very difficulty that Aquinas noticed, and takes it as a fundamental obstacle to the definition of truth as correspondence:

> A correspondence . . . can only be perfect if the corresponding things coincide and are, therefore, not distinct things at all. It is said to be possible to establish the authenticity of a bank note by comparing it stereoscopically with an authentic one. But it would be ridiculous to try to compare a gold piece with a twenty mark piece stereoscopically. It would only be possible to compare an idea with the thing if the thing were an idea too. And then, if the first did correspond perfectly with the second, they would coincide. But this is not at all what is wanted when truth is defined as correspondence of an idea with something real. For it is absolutely essential that the reality be distinct from the idea. But then there can be no complete correspondence, no complete truth. So nothing at all would be true; for what is only half true is untrue. (Frege [1918] 1967: 18–19)

Frege here raises a dilemma for the correspondence theorist: (a) either truth is a relation of identity between a representation and "something real" (but this is absurd, for it makes no sense to say that the representation and the thing are one and the same, whereas talk of correspondence implies that they are different), or (b) they are different, but then there can never be any full correspondence, in the sense of a coincidence, between the representation and the thing. In the second case, we would have to say that the two coincide *more or less*, or only to a certain degree. But this is equally absurd, for truth does not admit of degrees. Either a thought is true, or it isn't, and there are no intermediates. Now Frege has another argument, which is not only directed at the definition of truth as correspondence, but at *any* sort of definition:

> Cannot it be laid down that truth exists when there is correspondence in a certain respect? But in which? For what would we then have to do to decide whether something is true? We should have to enquire whether it is true that an idea and a reality, perhaps, corresponded in the laid-down respect. And we should be confronted by a question of the same kind and the game could begin again. So the attempt to explain truth as correspondence collapses. And every other attempt to define truth collapses too. For in a definition certain characteristics would have to be stated. And in application to any particular case the question would always arise whether it were true that the characteristics were present. So one goes round in a circle. Consequently, it is probable that the content of the word "true" is unique and indefinable. (Frege [1918] 1967: 19)

This second argument can be cast in the following way. Let us suppose that truth consists in a correspondence between some thought or judgement ("p") to some item in the world, a fact ("F"). So we shall define the truth of p as the obtaining of this relation ("C"):

(C1)   The thought that p is true iff $p\ C\ F$

Now the thought that $p\ C\ F$ should itself be true if the definition (C1) is to be correct. According to our definition, this should be cashed in terms of a correspondence between (C1) and a fact, which will presumably be a different fact from F, say F^*. So

(C2)   The thought that $p\ C\ F$ is true iff $p\ C\ F\ C\ F^*$

But for (C2) to be true, it has to correspond to a further fact, F^{**}. It is clear that here we embark on a regress, which can be called *Frege's* *regress.*[8] The argument can be generalized to *any* sort of relation which can be put in the place of correspondence. For instance, if C is the relation of *coherence* the argument will go through as well. It would go through too if we took truth to be an intrinsic property. Hence, concludes Frege, the content of the word "true" is indefinable, and if this word is to denote a relation or a property, these are equally indefinable. Actually Frege takes truth to be a property of thoughts (*Gedanken*), but he considers that it is impossible to define it.

This threatens a theory of truth as correspondence, but also any theory that would aim at giving a definition of truth. The regress argument can in fact be formulated in an even more general way, as a version of the "paradox of analysis". An analysis or a definition of truth is either vacuous – merely repeats in the definition what is to be defined – or it is informative and purports to be a genuine definition. In the first case, it is not a genuine definition, but an innocuous paraphrase. In the second case it cannot be a genuine definition either, because it will use the notion of truth in the *definiens*. This is illustrated by the definition of truth as correspondence with facts. Either to say that *p* is true "corresponds to the facts" is just another, empty, way of saying that *p* is true, or it really informs us about the content of "true". But it then has to be a *fact* that *p* corresponds to the facts, or that *p* corresponds to the facts is a fact. Unless we have an understanding of the notion of fact independent of our understanding of the notion of truth, such a definition tells us nothing. If an elucidation of truth in terms of correspondence with facts is not to be idle, one must deploy a notion of fact and of correspondence that would allow us to go further than the trivial equivalence between "It is true that *p*" and "it is a fact that *p*". It must provide a genuine account of facts as special kinds of entities that can be candidates for the relationship of *truth-making*.

Although the notion of fact as a primitive entity has been invoked by other philosophers, such as Aristotle (who perhaps meant something similar by the Greek word *pragma*), Leibniz, Brentano and his disciples Husserl and Reinach,[9] it has only gained philosophical prominence within early analytic philosophy, through Russell and through Wittgenstein's *Tractatus* when they developed the doctrines associated with "logical atomism". In his *Problems of Philosophy*,

Russell attempted to explain the truth of a judgement such as "Othello believes that Desdemona loves Cassio" as a relation of correspondence between the "propositional complex" *that Desdemona loves Cassio* and a complex entity in the world, made up of the individuals Desdemona and Cassio, and of the relation of love between them, something that we might express thus: <Desdemona, Cassio, loves>, where the items in this list are taken to be real things in the real world. So we can formulate this conception thus:

(Correspondence theory of facts)   *The proposition that* p *is true iff the fact* <p> *obtains*

where "<p>" stands for some complex entity made of individuals, properties or relations, and "obtains" is the holding of the appropriate correspondence relation. In some of his writings, Russell goes as far as to say that this entity, the fact <p>, *is* the very content of the judgement, that is, that the latter is constituted by the actual fact.[10] Here he seems to hold the view that truth is not the *correspondence* of a thought with a fact, but the *identity* between the two. Let us call this the *identity theory of facts*:

(Identity theory of facts)   *The proposition that* p *is true iff p and* <p> *are identical*

But there are two evident difficulties with each view. First, either it does not tell us anything about the content of the belief, or it makes it something different when the belief is false and when the belief is true. It seems hard to say that the *real* individuals and their relation are the constituents of the *judgement*. It would seem more reasonable to say that it is the individuals and the relation *as they are thought of*, that is, as mental entities, that are the object of the judgement.[11] The reason is obvious: the judgement may be false, while the subject may be related to the thought and its constituents nevertheless. And even if we take the constituents as real, we have no means to discern from the judgement itself, as constituted from the triple <Desdemona, Cassio, loves>, that the elements are ordered in the appropriate way: the individual may judge that Cassio loves Desdemona and thus be in contact with the three elements, but in the wrong way. Secondly, this difficulty also affects the view that the relation is not of identity but of correspondence: the view seems to be correct when the judgement is *actually* connected to this complex entity, but when it is false there is no such relation. In order to maintain his theory that truth involves a relation with a fact, Russell has to say that false judgements also involve such a relation, but with *negative facts*, or objective falsehoods. This sounds incredible.

Wittgenstein's version of logical atomism avoids these difficulties. He holds a correspondence theory of truth, where propositions represent or picture reality, and where the elements of propositions – which are ultimately names – correspond to the elements of reality – ultimately objects. Wittgenstein avoids the difficulties of Russell's theory of judgement first by distinguishing facts (*Tatsache*) from *states of affairs* (*Sachverhalte*). States of affairs are the merely possible correspondents of propositions, which, when they are true, correspond to facts. Hence facts are only the truth-makers of *true* propositions. Second, there are no negative facts (*Tractatus*, 4.25) in particular because in the proposition "not *p*" the logical constant "not" does not represent anything. Reality is only made up of elementary or atomic positive facts. Third, the correspondence relation between propositions and facts is characterized as a structural isomorphism between propositions and states of affairs. But when the relation between proposition and state of affairs obtains, or is realized – that is, when the proposition is true and denotes a fact – it is something that can only be shown, and cannot be said. So in the end, the correspondence relation is itself ineffable. This avoids Frege's regress, for we do not have to say that when *p* is true, it is *a fact* that *p* corresponds to a fact. But it only avoids it at the price of making the relation unexplainable.

In general, the trouble with a correspondence conception of truth couched in terms of facts is that it is very difficult to understand the nature of these entities independently of our understanding of the content of judgements or propositions to which they are supposed to correspond, and that it seems very hard to individuate facts if they are only defined as what makes propositions true. A well-known, although much disputed, argument, the "Frege–Gödel slingshot", tends to show this.[12] One true proposition, for instance that Amalfi is south of Naples, corresponds to what we might call its "personal" fact, *that Amalfi is south of Naples*, but also a number of less personal facts: for instance the fact *that Naples is north of Amalfi*, and also, since the following proposition is equivalent to the previous ones, to the fact *that Amalfi is south to the largest city within 30 miles of Ischia*, and also, since this is also equivalent, to the fact *that Amalfi is south to the largest city within 30 miles of Ischia and such that Tegucigalpa is the capital of Honduras*. But what does this latter fact have to do with the fact that Amalfi is south of Naples? In what way is it a truth-maker of the original truth? How can one avoid the personal fact, which is the truth-maker of p, burgeoning into a number of quite alien facts, or into a single huge conjunctive fact? This argument, which is a direct descendent of Frege's view that all true propositions name the True (and which can be expressed as saying that all true propositions have only one truth-maker, the Great Fact that is the World itself), seems to be fatal to any correspondence theory of facts. It challenges the friend of facts to escape from a dilemma: if all true propositions correspond to the same fact, the notion is useless, and if every proposition corresponds to a distinct fact, then the notion becomes idle, since facts just become, as David Armstrong puts it, "the tautological accusatives" of true propositions (Armstrong 1997: 19).[13]

Another argument has been advanced by Putnam (1983). It involves a complex theorem of model theory (the Löwenheim–Skolem theorem), but we can formulate it in the following way. If we grant that there is a world that is independent of our thoughts in the way a correspondence theory requires, then there have to be a large number of relations that hold between it and our thoughts or assertions. Putnam shows that if the world contains infinitely many elements, there must be many alternative ways of mapping the world onto our thoughts or assertions, which are just as systematic as the relation of correspondence is said to be. But how can we pick out these relationships and decide that it is the one that we intend to talk about when we talk about correspondence? Putnam takes this to refute the "absolute conception of reality", or the "external" or "transcendent" realist conception of truth. His argument has strong affinities with another well known argument in contemporary philosophy, Quine's thesis of the "inscrutability of reference". Given one way of mapping words onto things there are in principle many other non-equivalent ways of doing this, all compatible with the data. These arguments are controversial. But it is clear that they make life less easy for a correspondence theory.[14]

Two strategies, however, are still open to the partisans of a correspondence theory of facts. They can either try to provide more stringent conditions of individuation of facts, or simply accept that the notion of fact is bound to remain vague. A number of versions of the first strategy exist. They all have to resist in some way the slingshot argument, and to give a more fine-grained notion of fact, avoiding the classical difficulties examined above.[15] A related tradition consists in elaborating the Leibnizian–Husserlian notion of truth-maker.[16] The first step in order to avoid the problem of making facts the tautological accusatives of truths consists in allowing *other* entities than facts, and distinct from them, to be truth-makers; we saw an instance of this in Wittgenstein. Ramsey, in his criticism of Russell, takes this step. He says that what makes it true that Caesar died is not the fact that Caesar died, but the *event* of his death, an insight rediscovered by Davidson in his analysis of action sentences (Ramsey [1930] 1990: 37, Mulligan *et al.* 1984: 295, Davidson 1967). An individual event is a particular, not a fact. To see the difference, one can reflect that one does not say that Caesar's death is true, and that one can say that his death had a cause, whereas the fact that he died has no cause. The trouble with this proposal is that it is not clear that one can specify the event without describing it as a fact such as "the event of Caesar dying", or "the event such that Caesar died", and that not all sentences refer to events (for instance, an identity such as $a = a$ is not made true by an event or a state of affairs, but by an object), so one has to expand the ontology of truth-makers to include objects, states, processes, abstract particulars or "tropes", and so on.

Rather than attempting to describe the possible ontologies necessary for such views, let us consider here only Armstrong's (1997) theory, which belongs to this tradition. He also rejects the idea that each truth has its own personal truth-maker. On Armstrong's version of the correspondence theory of facts the truth-making relation is not one–one, but one–many or many–one. To take simple examples, if p or q (inclusive *or*) is true, this truth has two truth-makers, p and q. Or for a true existential sentence saying that there is at least one black swan, there are as many truth-makers as there are black swans. Conversely, one truth-maker corresponds to many truths. For instance, if it is true that either p or q is true, then the truth-maker for p is also a truth-maker for the disjunctive truth, and for innumerably many other truths (Armstrong 1997: 129–30). Although this avoids the second horn of the slingshot dilemma above, it hardly avoids the first: for the last example shows there can be one truth-maker for many truths, and in the end the world itself becomes the truth-maker of all truths.[17] But the main difficulty with Armstrong's theory of truth-makers, and other theories of this kind, is not so much the profligate metaphysics of states of affairs, universals and their individuation conditions that it presupposes. It is that such theories can hardly tell us why truth-makers "make" propositions true, hence explaining the correspondence relation, without presupposing the notion of a true proposition itself. To see this, consider what Armstrong calls "the truth-maker principle":

> The truth-maker for a truth must necessitate that truth. In the useful if theoretically misleading terminology of possible worlds, if a certain truth-maker makes a certain truth true, then there is no alternative world where that truth-maker exist but the truth is a false proposition. (1997: 115)

It is not clear that this does not amount to more than the truism that if a proposition is true then necessarily there is something in virtue of which it is true. In the sense of "necessity" in which this is an analytic truth, this is just a rephrasing of the definition of truth as correspondence. That does not tell *how* the "in virtue of" relation is instantiated, or how the truth-makers necessitate the truths. Now, if we formulate the principle as saying that every truth is necessitated by something, and if we read the necessity as a metaphysical necessity (*de re* necessity, as modal logicians call it, and not *de dicto* necessity):

(TM) necessarily if the proposition that p is true, then there is something such that it necessarily entails the truth of p

it implies both that a false proposition p necessarily has no truth-maker *and* that there is necessarily an infinity of possible truth-makers for p. For instance, if one says that a particle lacks spatial location at time t, the sentence "This particle is somewhere at t" is false (no truth-maker), but there is an infinity of possible places that the particle could have occupied, hence an infinity of possible truth-makers for the proposition.[18] This recalls the difficulty that Russell had with negative facts. One can avoid this consequence if TM is read as saying that

(TM*)   Necessarily if p then there is a proposition x such that this proposition is true and necessarily the truth of x implies that p

But this amounts to saying that necessarily a proposition that p is true if and only if p, and the notion of truth-making disappears. As we shall see in Chapter 2, this truism does not license any substantive notion of fact or state of affairs. But not all truth-makers theorists accept the principle (TM). This means that the truth-maker relation cannot be symmetric, unlike the relation of correspondence: the truth-makers necessitate the truths, but not all truths have their truth-makers. In this sense truth-making explains the "fit" between reality and truth, but this fit is not a genuine correspondence. The best way to understand the theory of truth-makers is to understand it not as a theory of *truth*, but as a theory of *being*, or an ontology. What it says is that all matters of truth depend, or supervene, on being, in the sense that there cannot be any difference in truths without difference in what there is. But the proper theory of truth that goes with this ontology has still to be specified.[19]

Austin (1950) opts for the second strategy. He takes truth-bearers to be statements, and not sentences or propositions. A statement is what a sentence says in a particular circumstance of its utterance. Statements are tied to the world through two kinds of conventions: (a) descriptive conventions, which correlate the words, in their ordinary use, with the types of situations, things and events that are to be found in the world, and (b) demonstrative conventions, which correlate words, in particular occasions of use, to the "historic" (or specific) situations found in the world. The first kind are roughly the conventions that determine the linguistic meaning of a word and associate it with a reference ("cat" is standardly used to denote cats), and the second are the conventions that determine how a particular word is used on an occasion ("cat" used on a particular occasion to denote a feline animal). Thus a statement is true when the historic state of affairs to which it is correlated by the demonstrative conventions is sufficiently similar to the standard states of affairs with which the sentence used in making it is correlated by the descriptive conventions. For instance "the cat is on the mat" is true when it is uttered in circumstances that fall roughly under the cat-being-on-the-mat type. Apart from the acknowledged vagueness in the notion of "standard states of affairs", what is odd in this account is the talk of conventions: they govern language, not what the world is, and they are arbitrary; so how can they tell us anything about how our statements relate to reality? But if we leave that aside, Austin's account does not go farther than a mere triviality: it just says that a statement is true when the relevant state of affairs is as it is said to be in the given circumstances.

So it seems that the correspondence theory of truth cannot articulate the notions of correspondence and of fact in a substantial, non-trivial way. It stumbles always on the difficulty that we cannot say much more than that: a thought or statement is true when the way the world is happens to be just as it says it is. This seems undeniable, and in this sense the correspondence, or the realist intuition, is inescapable. But the difficulty goes further. Saying more implies, as Russell, Wittgenstein and all the friends of facts have stressed, displaying an identity or a similarity of structure between the content of our thoughts and the way the world is itself structured. But when we want to articulate the world's structure, we seem not to be able to say anything more than that it corresponds to the structure of our thoughts. As Strawson, who has perhaps expressed this idea the most forcefully, says: "The only plausible candidate for what (in the world) makes a statement true is the fact it states; but the fact it states is not something in the world" (Strawson 1950: 195).

It is often said that these difficulties are due to a specific prejudice of the analytic school in philosophy: it focuses on linguistic or quasi-linguistic entities, such as sentences, statements or propositions, and tends to forget that we meet the world through other sorts of intermediaries than propositions and their like, such as sensations, perceptions, and experiences, which may not be propositional in nature. But will the problems disappear if instead of the contents of thoughts, judgements and propositions we concentrate on percepts? No, for in so far as we take these to be *representations*, the problem of their correspondence with reality will arise in just the same way, as the Cartesian and empiricist tradition of "ideas" as "pictures" or "copies" of reality amply shows. The only alternative seems to be to abandon the idea that our representations are an intermediary between us and the world, and hence any attempt to specify how they can hook onto things. But then, either we leave out the notion of a world that would be completely independent of our thoughts, or we accept that the world is "here", or "given" to us, but like an invisible photograph, to which we have no access. In the latter case, it is a version of what Wilfrid Sellars (1963) denounced as "the myth of the given". In the former case, as we shall see, it is difficult to avoid a form of idealism.

1.3 Coherence

The difficulties of articulating the relationship between truth and reality invite the following consideration: if any attempt to spell out the structure of facts brings us back to the structure of our thoughts and of the sentences that we use to express them, can there be a reality that would be independent from our judgements and of our interpretations? This leads to a familiar idea: to see a situation as a "fact" is to judge and interpret it, and our conceptual powers permeate and condition our experiences. If the facts "of" the world cannot be articulated apart from the way *we* structure the world, how can we tell what they are apart from a perspective from *within* our thoughts? When one's judgements confront experience, one does not reach reality itself, but further judgements, further beliefs, further statements. This, of course, invites a form of idealism or anti-realism, as against the realist picture that has driven us so far. If this idealism is not to be a mere form of Protagorean relativism or of Berkeleyan subjective idealism, it must say how truth can be an objective feature nevertheless. This can be provided, perhaps, by defining truth as a different sort of relation from correspondence, a relation of *coherence*.

This leads us to the coherence theory of truth: a thought, belief, or statement is true if and only if it appropriately belongs to a coherent set of propositions, beliefs and statements:

(Coherence)   X *is true iff* X *appropriately belongs to a coherent*
              set S

where "S" is meant to be a set of entities of the same kind as X. It is
important to add here the adverb "appropriately", in order to dispel
an obvious objection. If one understands "coherence" in the minimal
sense of the non-contradiction between a set of statements or beliefs,
it is clear that a lot of such sets will pass the test, which may nevertheless contain a lot of intuitively false beliefs. Actually any otherwise
coherent fictional story may contain non-contradictory but false
beliefs. Moreover any coherent set of beliefs can be made more
coherent by adding to it one or more false beliefs, and there can be
rival and divergent belief systems that are all internally coherent.
This is the objection that Russell addressed to the coherence theory:
the proposition that Bishop Stubbs was hanged for murder is false,
but it can become true if it is included in a sufficiently coherent and
comprehensive set of other propositions. The question is: which set?
and how to determine it?[20] To this coherentists about truth answer
that what they mean by "coherence" among a set of beliefs is that the
beliefs must be in some sense *controlled*, or *justified* by a certain
criterion or *pedigree* that they share. In this sense, when we say that
the beliefs of a single person, or of a whole community, are coherent, what is required is not that they should *all* be coherent (if we
could draw a list of them), but that a *weighted majority* of them be
such. Talk of a pedigree, a test, or a criterion of coherence means that
the coherence relation must be an epistemic one, and in this sense the
coherence theory is an *epistemic* conception of truth, one that in
some sense gives an *explanation* of the relation (hence the word
"appropriately" in the foregoing definition). For this reason, the
relation in question will be a matter of degree, and it may also be in
some sense context-relative (since explanation is a context-relative
notion), and coherence theorists may take truth as coherence to
depend upon the subject matter. For instance, one might accept the
view that moral truths are such in virtue of some sort of coherence,
although this does not apply to empirical or scientific truths, or that
theoretical statements in science have to be coherent, in contrast
with empirical statements. There can be such combinations within
the doctrine of a single philosopher. For instance, Kant holds some
sort of coherence view for concepts, or for the categories of the

understanding, whereas what he calls "intuitions" or the deliverance of sense experience are not subject to such a criterion. Such views would, however, hardly qualify as candidates for full-blown coherentism, but only as local versions of it, since they accept that truth could be understood in the correspondentist sense in some regions. Full-blown coherentism is a different kind of view. It is the view that we can integrate into a maximally coherent whole larger and larger sets of our beliefs, so that in the end we reach a complete system. A first extension might involve the consideration not of our actual beliefs, but also of what we *would* believe in future or in ideal circumstances, or, as Peirce would say, at "the end of human enquiry". We might extrapolate even more by supposing that the maximal coherence state is reached only within the beliefs of God or of an Absolute Mind. In this sense various philosophical views, such as Spinoza's pantheistic monism or Hegel or Bradley's absolute idealism, will be paradigm examples of full-blown coherentism.

Let us suppose that we could understand such idealizations, and that truth can only be predicated of beliefs integrated into such comprehensive wholes as Nature, God, Substance, or the Absolute. Then, as Bradley made clear, truth could never be predicated of a single belief, but only of the Absolute system, since no truth is ever a perfect truth. Hence all our beliefs, apart from those about the Absolute, are only conditionally true, or true only to a degree.[21] Contrary to what Frege said, truth will be a matter of degree. But when we have reached the ideal state, how can we say that we have reached Truth, if not because it is supposed to reflect – to *correspond* to or to be *identical* with – the whole of reality? It is not clear here that the talk of an ideally coherent system does not collapse into the idea of an ideally *corresponding* system that is *about* reality. Neither is it clear that the system in question has to be mental, or made of mind stuff. Spinoza's *Deus sive natura*, or nature according to the doctrines of "emergentism" of the end of the nineteenth century, such as Samuel Alexander's (1920), as an evolving system going from brute matter to a Mind that will, in the end, be God's, are not solely mental wholes. The official coherentist's view is that truth is a relation between thoughts. But it is very difficult for the coherentist to avoid saying that when the appropriate test of coherence is met the thoughts are simply true, in the correspondence sense. We are thus led to suspect that, far from defining truth, the coherence conception of truth as ideal or absolute justification of our beliefs actually presupposes the concept of truth.

Now, although coherentism has often been associated in the history of philosophy with the high-flown metaphysical doctrines of absolute idealism or monism, there is no necessity in this. And there does seem to be an intuition at the root of the doctrine that is worth spelling out: that a given belief is true only if it can be *justified*, or *warranted* in a certain way, and that truth has an essential connection to *knowledge*. The coherentist takes this justification to be tied not only to individual beliefs, but to systems of beliefs, hence holds the view that knowledge is also a matter of coherence. But here again, it is not necessary, and there will be coherentist as well as non-coherentist versions of *epistemic* theories of truth.

1.4 Verificationism

An epistemic theory of truth is one that essentially ties truth to our epistemic justification for beliefs: truth is a matter of whether a belief is justified, warranted, rational, acceptable, and so on. Roughly, the schema here is:

(Epistemic theory)   X *is true iff* X *satisfies some epistemic condition*

In this sense a definition of truth for such theories is inseparable from a *criterion* of truth. But it need not straightforwardly assimilate truth to justification. For one might have a criterion of truth without this criterion being a definition of truth itself. Thus the catalogue of a library gives us a criterion for the presence or the absence of a book in the library, but what we mean when we say that the book is in the library is not that the book is in the catalogue.[22] Or take Descartes's view. His criterion for truth is self-evidence or the clarity and distinctiveness of our ideas, but his official definition of truth is the adequacy of ideas with respect to things. Another reason why truth does not simply amount to justification is that justification is context-relative and defeasible: one can have a justification for p at t and in circumstances c, but cease to be justified at t' and in c'. The justification must be in some sense stable and undefeasible.

We have seen that coherentism, in so far as it defines truth as the coherence of a set of beliefs constrained by an epistemic condition, qualifies as an epistemic theory of truth. But the most common kind of epistemic theory of truth is *verificationism*: it identifies the truth of a statement with its verifiability:

(Verificationism)   X *is true iff* X *is verifiable*

This should not be confused with a verificationist theory of *meaning*. The latter says that the meaning of a statement or sentence is the method by which we verify it. The possession of a method – for instance, checking one's memories – for establishing the meaning of a certain sentence about the past need not imply that such sentences are true when so verified. But there is a link between the first and the second, for when the method is conclusive and reliable – if memory were so reliable, for instance, by giving us direct acquaintance with past events – the method of verification warrants the truth of the statement. The link appears better in the other direction: if one equates the meaning of a sentence with its *truth conditions*, and if the truth conditions are the verification conditions, then one can move from a verificationist conception of truth to a verificationist conception of meaning.[23]

The logical positivists tried to defend such verificationist conceptions of meaning and of truth in the 1930s, on the basis of an empiricist epistemology according to which the meaning of a statement and its truth could be ascertained from its connections to experiences. On this basis they drew a distinction between those statements that are true on the basis of our verifications by sense experience (synthetic) and those that are true purely in virtue of meaning and linguistic conventions alone (analytic truths). Notoriously, these accounts failed because of their reductionist character: the task of isolating purely empiricist criteria for the meaningfulness and truth of our beliefs is hopeless. As a number of critics of this empiricist conception, including logical positivists such as Hempel or Neurath, and in particular Quine, have shown, the meaning of an individual isolated statement or belief, and hence its truth (if the truth of a statement depends upon what we take it to mean) cannot be ascertained independently from a background of other statements, and thus cannot be reduced to basic empirical tests. Here we stumble again on a feature upon which the coherentist conception of truth insisted: the *holism* or the necessarily network-connected character of our beliefs. In the philosophy of science, the problem for a verificationist conception of the truth of scientific theories is familiar: rival and incompatible theories can predict exactly the same empirical consequences. Theories are underdetermined by the possible evidence. This leads to the view, known as the Duhem–Quine thesis, that only whole theories meet experience, and not isolated beliefs, and that appropriate adjustments can always be made to make them fit the data. But then this coherence theory of knowledge will again stumble upon the difficulty that affects the coherence theory of truth, that one can always enlarge, or modify, our coherent sets of beliefs to adapt them to reality.

But perhaps we can save the basic insights of the verificationist conception of meaning and truth without endorsing its most reductionist and coherentist consequences. This is what philosophers like Dummett (1978, 1991) have tried to show. Dummett's programme aims at giving us a new framework for thinking about the issues that traditionally oppose, in philosophy, realism and anti-realism. He claims that these issues do not concern so much the kind of entities that we can consider as "real" or not, but the kind of *conception of truth* that underlies our commitments. Realism and anti-realism are thus primarily *semantic* theses. Dummett starts from a reflection on the meaning and the truth of mathematical statements. The view known as Platonism in the philosophy of mathematics says that they are true in virtue of some independent reality, which will exist whether we are able to recognize it or not. So Platonism not only embodies a "realist" conception of truth, but also a realist conception of meaning, according to which the meaning of mathematical statements "transcends" their possible verification. The opposite view, constructivism, says that they do not transcend this verification, and equates truth with proof or demonstration. For it, the meaning of a statement will be given by its *assertibility* (or proof) conditions.

Dummett's conception can be thought of as an attempt to extend this opposition from the mathematical case to the case of the meaning of other sorts of statements than mathematical ones, hence to provide a theory of meaning for whole languages that would be based on constructivistic assumptions. But if so, it would presuppose a certain conception of truth and meaning instead of being an attempt to *show*, on independent grounds, that such a conception is correct. So his considered view is rather that a verificationist theory of truth can be established on the basis of a verificationist theory of meaning. To defend the latter, he argues that a language could not be learnt, nor the meanings of its sentences be made manifest to others, if one could not associate with them specifiable assertion-conditions, or, to take up Wittgenstein's slogan that "meaning is use", use-conditions. He claims that we have no conception of what various "recognition-transcendent" sentences, about the past, about counterfactual circumstances, or about remote regions of space and time could be, although we understand such sentences, hence that what we mean by such sentences cannot be their "realistic" truth conditions. He is thus led to propose an "anti-realist" semantics in terms of assertibility conditions, which is a version of the verificationist view:

(Warranted assertibility)   X *is true iff* X *is warrantedly assertible*

As Dummett puts it in "Truth",

> We no longer explain the sense of a statement by stipulating its truth-value in terms of the truth-values of its constituents, but by stipulating when it may be asserted in terms of the conditions under which its constituents may be asserted.
>
> ([1959] 1978: 17–18)

But such an epistemic, or verificationist, theory of meaning will not leave untouched our ordinary conception of truth. This can be seen for the simple case of negation. In classical logic, "it is not true that p" and "not-p" have the same meaning. But if truth is warranted assertibility, "p" means "It is assertible that p", and "not-p" means "It is not assertible that p". But "It is not assertible that p" is not equivalent to "It is assertible that not-p" (for instance, that we have no evidence that the Loch Ness monster exists does not mean that we have evidence that it does not exist). At some point, such an anti-realist semantics will have to reject (or to suspend belief in) the classical principle of *bivalence*, that every statement is either true or false, *tertium non datur*.

So it seems that a radically epistemic conception of meaning will do more than give a definition of truth in terms of epistemic access, but also that it will revise our ordinary concept of it. Such a conception embodies two problematic assumptions. The first is that one could give verification conditions one by one, for each kind of sentences. In the light of the holistic character of verification, this is dubious. The second is that a verificationist theory of meaning leads to a verificationist theory of truth: truth *is* warranted assertibility. But warranted assertibility is not truth, for this goes against our best realistic intuitions: it seems perfectly possible to have all the best justifications for the truth of a statement, although this statement might be false. What is true may not coincide with what is *known* to be true. Now could we suppose that we can reach a stage where a statement, or a set of statements, are such that they can completely be justified in an *ideal* situation? We have already seen that this idealization move is characteristic of the coherence theory of truth. But we have also seen that when it is supposed to imply that we reach the standpoint of an omniscient being or an absolute conception of reality, this conception is dubiously an anti-realist or epistemic conception of truth. So the ideal state is better constructed as that of an ideal knower, who would, in relevant respects, be like *us*, but who would, also in relevant respects, be unlike us. Putnam (1983), after Peirce, has once proposed such a view of truth as "idealized rational acceptability" (or warranted assertibility): a belief is true if and only if it would be justifiable in a situation where all the relevant evidence were available.

(Ideal Warranted Assertibility)   X *is true iff* X *would be warrantedly assertible (believed) in ideal conditions*

There are a number of objections to such a view. The most obvious is that we have no idea of what these epistemically ideal circumstances and of what the "relevant evidence" might be, and that we do not see how such beliefs could be justified if they were not *true*. This view also leads to paradoxical consequences, which have been made manifest by Frederic Fitch (1963) and Alvin Plantinga (1982).[24] Fitch's argument is the "paradox of knowability":

The paradox of knowability. (a) If something is true, then it is at least knowable, even if it is, *de facto*, unknown. (b) Moreover it is possible that there are truths that are unknown and will never be known (*i.e* unknowable truths).(c) But if something is an unknowable truth, then it is possible for it to be known (by (a)). So (d) if something is known to be an unknowable truth, then it is known to be a truth; but if it is known to be an unknowable truth then it *is* an unknowable truth, and hence it is not known. So it is impossible that there could be a truth that will never be known, and if there is an unknowable truth, it will never be known to be such.

How does that bear on ideal verificationism? Substitute in the previous argument "believed to be true in ideal circumstances" for "true". It follows that if something cannot be believed under ideal circumstances, it can never be believed that it is so in the ideal circumstances. So the biconditional expressing ideal warranted assertibility above fails to be true when "X" is "X cannot be believed under ideal circumstances". I shall not detail Plantinga's argument, which attacks the claim, made by the ideal verificationist, that truth cannot outrun possible justification. It shows that it does not have the resources to assert that the circumstances are not ideal: it is a necessary truth that the circumstances are ideal.

Such difficulties have led Putnam to renounce the thesis that truth could be defined as ideal justification, and to retreat to the view that they are interdependent. So, as with metaphysical coherentism, the definition actually presupposes the notion of truth (Putnam 1990: 115).

1.5 Pragmatism
Prima facie, the so-called pragmatist conceptions of truth do not belong to the same family as those that we have examined so far, for they are generally taken to define truth in terms of a different sort of relation from correspondence or coherence, which, moreover, does not seem to be epistemic: they define the truth of a belief in terms of its utility or of its beneficial consequences for action:

(Pragmatist theory)   X *is true iff* X *is useful*

No historical pragmatist, however, expressed this view in this crude form. James is sometimes close to it when he says that:

> "The true" . . . is only the expedient in the way of our thinking, just as 'the right' is the expedient in the way of our behaving", and that "the true is the name of whatever proves itself to be good in the way of belief and good, too, for definite assignable reasons" (James 1907: 106; 1909: 42).

Peirce disclaimed strongly that he had defended a doctrine about truth similar to James's. His own "pragmatic maxim" was not aimed at a definition of truth, but a complex methodological rule: "Consider what effects, that might conceivably have practical bearings, we conceive the object of our conception to have. Then, our conception of these effects is the whole of our conception of the object" (Peirce 1935–58, vol. V: 402). If we set aside the actual pragmatists' views, the crude pragmatist "definition" above is open to evident objections, which have been voiced by Russell in his criticism of James.[25] There are many beliefs that are useful, but false, and vice versa. Moreover the doctrine has an air of subjectivism or relativism: what is useful for X might not be useful for Y, and at least depends upon our desires and goals, which are not obviously reduced to a single one, and on the circumstances. Worse, as Russell remarks, pragmatism, so understood, completely misrepresents the concept of knowledge: to know that p is to know that p is true, not to know that p is useful. Just as Mill complained about purely hedonistic interpretations of utilitarianism, James bitterly complained against narrow interpretations of his views. He protested that he did not want to defend the philistine view that the truth of a belief is its mere "cash value" or the fact that "it pays", but that he wanted to locate the meaning and importance of truth in our intellectual life, and to attract attention to how much purely intellectual ideals (the "disinterested search for truth") are connected to practical ideals, to emotional life and to action in general. But then it becomes unclear that pragmatism offers a definition of truth at all, instead of reflections on the *point* of a notion of truth. At best, utility is a *criterion* of truth, and Russell here was right to suspect that James might have confused it with a definition. Pragmatism in general is better construed as a certain conception of *belief* rather than as a distinctive conception of truth.

Peirce bases pragmatism (which he preferred to call "pragmaticism" to avoid the philistine implications), upon the thesis that belief is a *disposition to act*. To believe that *p* is to be disposed to act in certain ways, or to acquire certain habits of mind. This might, provided appropriate ways of fixing the desires of agents and their kinds of behaviour, give a definition of beliefs, but it can hardly give us a definition of their truth, for this definition presupposes that, for an action to be the successful realization of our desires (and provided we can know their contents), the beliefs in question have to be *true*. For instance the reason why it is useful for me to believe that I am sitting on a chair is that, on the face of my perceptions, I feel at this moment that I am sitting on it. This is certainly a useful belief, since if I did not have it, I would not be able to sit and write, which are for the moment useful actions. But the truth *that I am now sitting* is not for that constituted by the utility of these actions. Rather it is *because* the belief is true that the actions are useful. In fact my utility is exactly a function of my capacity to react to an objective world upon which my beliefs inform me, and not the other way round.

The interesting doctrine in pragmatism, which was developed by Ramsey, who considered himself to be Peirce's disciple, is not one about truth, but one about the *meanings* of our beliefs: their meaning, or their truth conditions, are their *utility conditions*, the way in which they *generally* (although they might not in particular circumstances) lead to successful actions in the long run. This is called, in contemporary philosophy, a "success semantics" for beliefs,[26] and there is a biological evolutionist version of it: on a large scale those of our beliefs that are true are those that tend to be beneficial for our species (this is called "teleosemantics"[27]). That can provide us with a realistic conception of meaning and representation (which can be considered as an appropriate alternative to Dummett's anti-realist conception considered above), but it does not define truth in biological and functional terms. Rather the biologically reductive story employs a realistic and correspondentist definition of truth as the property (useful by all means) to represent the environment.

Peirce himself was an evolutionist, but his pragmatism had a more idealist twist. His own view of truth is, as I have already noted, best understood as a form of ideal coherentism or ideal verificationism:

our beliefs are true when they are held "at the limit of scientific enquiry" by a community of researchers.[28] At this limit, the beliefs will have achieved their maximum utility, but it is an intellectual utility, for a kind of action that is scientific action. This is a combination of the ideal warranted assertibility view and of the pragmatist "definition". But it does not say that the ideal condition follows from the pragmatist definition. Rather, it says that the latter would follow from the former. Once we have reached the ideal limit, it cannot but prove useful for knowledge (and so it is a special kind of *epistemic* utility which is aimed at). It is also essential for Peirce that the progress of scientific enquiry oriented towards this ideal limit be a process of *revision* and criticism of our beliefs. We might, within this process, as James insisted in his famous paper "The Will to Believe" (1897), accept certain views for which we temporarily do not have sufficient evidence for their truth, but that we find useful for later stages of the enquiry (we shall come back to this doctrine below, §4.5). But these beliefs cannot be assessed for other reasons than the fact that we take them as true. And at the end of scientific enquiry, the overall coherent set of our beliefs will just be *true*. But we have already seen the difficulties that such a view encounters.

The foregoing indicates that there are many varieties of pragmatism: some, when they amount to a form of coherentism, are closer to idealism and epistemic theories of truth; others, when they include a conception of an ideal correspondence to reality and a realistic view of truth conditions, are closer to realism; and some others, as we shall see, flirt with relativism. We shall meet again the ideal limit conception. But for the moment, we can conclude that pragmatism is at best a fairly unstable conception of truth.[29]

1.6 The identity theory

At several stages we have met the view that truth might not be a relation between our thoughts and reality or between thoughts and facts, but a relation of *identity* between them. As we have seen, this is one way of reading Aristotle's famous dictum in *Metaphysics* (Γ 1011b, 26). It might also underlie some medieval views, as when Anselm of Canterbury identified truth with God (*De Veritate*: 151–74). As we saw, Frege contemplated an identity theory of truth in the course of his argument against correspondence, and Russell tended to assimilate true propositions with facts. We have formulated above the identity theory of facts. Identity would be a limiting case of correspondence. But it might also be a limiting case of coherence too, when the whole integrated set of our thoughts *is* the Absolute or Being. There is a more general definition, which might accommodate this compatibility with a correspondence as well as a coherence conception:

(Identity theory of truth)   X *is true iff* X *is identical to reality*

Such a view is sometimes called an *identity* theory of truth. Although it captures a long-standing intuition, and was present from the very beginnings of analytic philosophy, the identity theory of truth has received attention only recently, and it is a relative newcomer in these discussions.[30] It has an air of Eleatic, deep-sounding doctrine. But is it clear that it makes sense and that it forms a distinctive conception of truth that might be added to the preceding list?

The identity theory hardly makes sense when truth-bearers are taken to be sentences. How can a mere series of sounds or symbols be identical with a piece of reality? The same implausibility affects the view that the truth-bearers are mental entities, for their identification to reality sounds like Berkeleyan idealism (*esse est percipi*). The only way to construe them meaningfully is to say that the *contents* of thoughts is the appropriate candidate for the identification.[31] Moore, in his early period, defended such a view against a correspondence theory:

> So far, indeed, from truth being defined by reference to reality, reality can only be defined by reference to truth: for truth denotes exactly the property of the complex formed by two entities and their relation, in virtue of which, if the entity predicated the existence, we call the complex real – the property, namely, expressed by saying that the relation in question does truly or really hold between the entities.   (Moore 1901: 21)

Moore holds that reality consists in true *propositions*, and in the concepts of which they are made of, that is of the complexes and the properties that true thoughts *are identical to*. But this can be read as much as a statement of extreme realism as it can be read as a state-ment of extreme idealism.[32] If one remembers our above discussion of the notion of fact, the steps of this dialectic can be followed easily. We start by asking: to what can true thoughts be identified? To particular facts? If we do not want to countenance negative facts, we shall have to say that the identity holds only for true thoughts. But then the identity theory of truth comes close to a truism: a thought that p is true when *it is a fact* that p, or when the fact that p holds. In this truistic sense, the identity theory is hardly a substantive view. It looks very similar to what we shall call in the next chapter a deflationist conception of truth.[33] Now, when the facts are not appropriately individuated, we have to say that all true thoughts are identical with one Fact, the Big Fact of Reality itself. The identity, or equivalence constitutive of an identity theory of truth – a true thought *is* a fact, or a true thought is identical to real-ity – can be read in two ways, as in Moore's formulation. From right to left, this nudges thought into reality. From left to right, this nudges fact or reality into thought. The former is the identity theory of facts. The latter sounds like Absolute idealism. In this sense Spinoza or Hegel might be identity theorists of truth: Nature or Substance is One, seen from two aspects, Thought and Exten-sion, or the Real and the Rational coincide. In the sense in which Russell (1914) called "mysticism" the belief in the essential unity of reality and thought, or monism, the Identity theory of truth embod-ies a form of mysticism. The idea that thought and reality are identical when truth holds may be the last word about it, but as Bradley says, this deep intuition cannot be spelled out:

> I must venture to doubt whether . . . truth, if that stands for the work of the intellect, is ever precisely identical with fact . . . Such an idea might be senseless, such a thought might contra-dict itself, but it serves to give voice to an appropriate instinct.
> (Bradley 1922: 49–50).

In so far as it is a substantive view of truth, it seems that the identity theory is ineffable.

We have now reviewed the main substantive conceptions of truth present on the philosophical scene. The upshot of our discussion seems to be the following. In their attempts to give general and comprehensive definitions of truth, philosophers have not achieved much: either they have provided "theories" that fly in the face of obvious facts (justification is not truth, coherence is not enough, utility is not truth either), or they have not been able to go farther than mere platitudes (a thought is true when it tells us the way the world is). Every attempt to go further than such truisms either seems to beg the question (to presuppose the notion of truth) or to commit us to dubious metaphysical assumptions. Moreover, most of the theories that we have examined so far are unstable: it is very hard for each definition to be kept pure, for correspondence truth is difficult to defend without adding epistemic elements in it, and epistemic and coherence truth are hard to maintain without relying on some concept of correspondence, such as truth as utility, or truth as identity. This does not necessarily toll the death knell for a substantive and informative real definition of the *essence* of truth, for one might argue that such a definition does not have to agree with our most common *concept* of truth. After all a theory of X may reveal features that do not harmonize with our current notion of X. H_2O does not sound like "water", thoughts and feelings do not look like products of neuronal activity. But at least what one expects from a real sophisticated and possibly unintuitive definition is that it explains, like H_2O, the ordinary features of the *definiens*. But none of the definitions that we have considered does this. So perhaps Frege was right: truth is an indefinable property. It might even not be a *property* of anything at all. So it is time to explore option 2 in Figure 1.

2 Deflationism

In this chapter, I shall discuss various views on truth that have been called *deflationist*. They reject the idea that truth can be defined as a "robust" or "substantive" metaphysical notion, and claim that truth is not a genuine property: it is a simple, formal or logical, device of assertion, which does not amount to much more than the truism that *p* and *it is true that p* are equivalent. In other words, we empty the right-hand side in our (Def *T*) schemas of any genuine content, to keep only their bare logico-linguistic form, which is just:

X *is true iff* X

where the only candidate for the other side of the equivalence is simply *X* itself. But then the equivalence becomes trivial: the right-hand side does not tell us much, if anything. The upshot of such views is to deflate the notion of truth, to the effect that there is not much to say about it. But this simplicity, or this simple-mindedness, can, as we shall see, be deceptive.

2.1 Varieties of deflationism

Let us use the generic term *deflationism* to designate the family of views that can appropriately be placed under heading (2) in Figure 1 (p. 12). They all share two negative commitments. The first is that truth is not a genuine property or relation. The second is correlative: truth has no real essence or nature, and cannot be defined as such. This means that one cannot give any "substantive" or "robust" definition in the sense of the various "theories" examined in Chapter 1. But this does not mean that we cannot characterize, or in this looser sense define, our *concept* of truth, nor tell what it *means* in ordinary usage. Indeed most of these views rely on the ordinary use of the predicate "true". The point is that the predicate, if such there is, does not express a property, or a least a deep one. This is well brought out by Frege in a passage that seems to anticipate the deflationist option:

> The thought expressed in [the] words "that sea-water is salt" coincides with the sense of the sentence "that sea-water is salt". So the sense of the word "true" is such that it does not make any essential contribution to the thought. If I assert "It is true that sea-water is salt", I assert the same thing as if I assert "Sea-water is salt". This enables us to recognize that the assertion is not to be found in the word 'true' but in the assertoric force with which the sentence is uttered. This may lead us to think that the word "true" has no sense at all. But in that case a sentence in which "true" occurred would have no sense either. All that one can say is: the word "true" has a sense that contributes nothing to the sense of the sentence in which it occurs as a predicate.   (Frege 1979: 251–2)

This feature is sometimes called the *transparency* of the predicate "true": "'p' is true", "It is true that p" and "p" have the same meaning. Expressing the notion of equivalence by the biconditional relation "if and only if" (iff), we can formulate the following *Equivalence Principle*:

(E)   It is true that p iff p

But there are two ways of reading it. In (E), *that p* is supposed to stand for the *content* (or, as Frege says, the *sense*) of the sentence "*p*", that is, for the *proposition* that p. In another reading, it can stand for '*p*' itself, when the predicate "is true" is directly applied to the *sentence* "*p*", with the following formulation:

(DS)   "p" is true iff p

Here the sentence on the left is *quoted*, whereas the one on the right is *used*. (DS) is called the *disquotation* schema. This difference about the choice of truth-bearers is important. It marks the distinction between various *deflationist* views and *disquotationalism*, although the latter is also, in a broad sense, a deflationist conception. Disquotationalism, since it takes truth to be a predicate of sentences, seems to relativize it to a language. It has obvious affinities with Tarski's "semantic conception of truth", although, as we shall see, they differ. The species of deflationism that we can call *minimalism* says that truth is a mere device of assertion of propositions, which, to use Frege's characterization does not contribute to the sense of the propositions asserted. In its most radical forms, the *redundancy* and the *prosentential* conceptions of truth, it suggests that "true" could well be eliminated, in which case it would not even be a predicate. A characteristic expression of the redundancy view is Ayer's well-known statement in *Language, Truth and Logic*:

> We find that in all sentences of the form "*p* is true", the phrase "is true" is logically superfluous. When for example, one says that the proposition "Queen Anne is dead" is true, all that one is saying is that Queen Anne is dead. And similarly, when one says that the proposition "Oxford is the capital of England" is false, all that one is saying is that Oxford is not the capital of England. Thus, to say that a proposition is true is just to assert it, and to say that it is false is just to assert its contradictory. And this indicates that the terms "true" and "false" connote nothing, but function in the sentence simply as marks of assertion and denial. And in that case there can be no sense in asking us to analyse the concept of "truth".   (Ayer 1936: 117–18)

This gives us a complex map of what falls under the general heading of deflationism (Fig. 2).

2.2 Redundancy and disquotation

The idea that "true" is not a genuine *predicate* is suggested by the fact that "it is true that *p*" and "*p*" seem to say the same thing. Adding "It's true" to "*p*" seems to be merely a redundant[1] way of asserting that *p*. Ayer popularized this thesis, but Ramsey (in "Facts

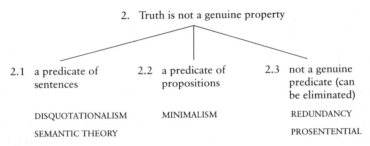

Figure 2

and Propositions", 1930) is often considered as its first exponent, and he was actually making this point against Russell's assimilation of propositions to facts: here the redundantist theory helps us to get rid of entities such as facts, for "It is a fact that p" just means p. When "true" seems to have a different meaning, it does not seem to add much *cognitive value*, as Frege would say, to the mere assertion that p, and it indicates merely the *force* of the assertion. When people add "That's true" to an assertion of p, they just seem to endorse it and to *express* their attitude, rather than *describing* anything. Because performative utterances such as "I apologize" have just this function, this is often called the *performative* conception of truth. Strawson (1950) held it once, and went as far as to say that "is true" *never* has a statement-making role and for this reason is not a property. But, as he later admitted, it does have this role, for instance in inferences, when from "What you said is true" and "You said that p" we infer p. In spite of this, a redundantist can still claim that "is true" can be eliminated from the statement-making contexts in which it figures. That seems possible when "is true" is predicated of individual sentences, but it poses a problem when it is predicated of groups of sentences, as in "What you said in your lecture was true", or "Everything that the Pope says is true" (which are sometimes called "blind" predications). Ramsey proposes the paraphrase:

(R)   "For all p, if he says that p, then p"[2]

But here the commitments of the redundancy theory arise. For the variable p, in its first occurrences seems to stand for a name, the name of a proposition, and not of a sentence. If we take it to be a sentence, we have to quantify over sentences and this would give:

(R*)   For all p, if he says "p", then p

But the consequent would make no sense unless we added to it "is true", so it would not eliminate it. It has been suggested that we could have recourse to substitutional quantification. But, apart from other problems, this kind of quantification is ordinarily interpreted in terms of truth, for "$(\exists x)\ Fx$" in the substitutional sense means "Some substitution instance of 'F . . .' is true", and so truth is reintroduced (Soames 1999: 40–2). Another proposal, elaborated by various authors,[3] suggests that we generalize from contexts of this sort:

(a)   Mary: There are a million stars out tonight
(b)   John: If it is true, then the sky is clear

and take the "it" in (b) to refer anaphorically to the utterance (a). "What you said was true" becomes "There is something such that you said that *it* is true, and it is true" (or, to use a device introduced by Arthur Prior, replacing "it is true" by an imaginary anaphoric pronoun *itt*, "There is something such that you said that *itt*, and itt"[4]). "It is true" here still occurs, but it functions like a pronoun (a quantificational pronoun standing for sentences) in a "prosentence", and thus it is not a categorematic expression with an independent meaning. This is why this is called the *prosentential* theory. But it does not make clear that "true" disappears, nor that we can dispense, with such accounts, of the notion of the content of what is said (which the pronoun "it" or "*itt*" abbreviates). All these views – redundancy, performative and prosentential – have been called "nihilist" or "disappearance" conceptions of truth. But they can eliminate completely neither the predicate "true" nor the notion of proposition.

A more promising way of dispensing with the latter is to consider truth as a *bona fide* predicate of *sentences*, and to opt for the schema (DS). For those philosophers who, like Quine, have a suspicion of entities like propositions, this seems the proper line to take. He says that the function of "true" is to enable us to quote a sentence by adding to it "is true":

"Snow is white" is true

as well as to "disquote" the result

Snow is white

without any loss. So truth is just a device of "semantic ascent" (from talk about the world to talk about language) or "semantic descent" (back from language to the world) (Quine 1990: 80–4). "True", as a semantic elevator, is a very convenient device, for, as Quine notes, instead of discussing the whiteness of snow, it allows us to switch to sentences, by discussing the truth of "snow is white". How does this disquotational conception deal with blind ascriptions of truth? "What you said is true" is equivalent to an infinite disjunction (or with the universal quantifier "All you say is true" an infinite conjunction):

> What you said = "Grass is green" and grass is green or what you said = "Snow is white" and snow is white or . . .

So we can generalize the disquotational schema (DS):

(DS*) x is true iff (x = "s_1" & s_1) or (x = "s_2" & s_2) or . . .

where "s_1", "s_2", . . . abbreviate sentences. The point, here, is not that "true" ceases to be a genuine predicate, or that it disappears, although (DS*) might be recruited at the service of this claim. But disquotationalists, unlike redundantists on this point, insist that "true" is a useful predicate, which allows us to refer, in group, to sets of sentences. If we did not have it, we would have to invent it. But it is in the spirit of this view that it is only a "device", not a deep word.

Since truth-bearers are here sentences, the schemas (DS) and (DS*) can apply even to sentences that we do not understand, either because they belong to an alien language, or because we cannot make sense of them. For instance "'Snarks are boojums' is true iff snarks are boojums" is a perfectly acceptable instance of (DS). This is odd, because if we ascribe truth to a sentence, it would seem that we should know what it means, or the proposition that it expresses. But the disquotationalist insists that it is an advantage of this view, for it shows that truth can be applied to sentences *in advance* of constructing what they mean, and that this brings out well the fact that it is a mere formal device of disquotation. A (DS)-type sentence, however, might be true in one language, but false in another.[5] Moreover, a number of sentences containing demonstratives or indexicals ("I'm hungry", "Tom is happy now") are true in one context and for one speaker, but false in another. More generally (and we shall come back to that) disquotationalism supposes that what the words in a quoted sentence *mean* remains fixed when one applies the predicate "true". But if the word "snow" had been used to designate mud, say, the sentence "snow is white" would have been false. Mere sentences are ill-suited as truth-bearers. Unless it is applied to what Quine calls "eternal sentences" (such as "2 + 2 = 4" or "Caesar invaded Gaul") or to sentences of which the meaning is fixed, the disquotational theory must be restricted to languages, speakers and idiolects. We could, of course, avail ourselves of the resources of translation of sentences from one language into another; but the notion of translation will presuppose the notion of synonymy or identity of meaning that the theory was supposed to avoid. So it seems to lack the appropriate generality needed to make it applicable to truth *in general*. Another way of expressing this difficulty is to remark that, on the disquotationalist view, (DS)-sentences are supposed to be necessary, or in some sense *a priori*, but that the relativity of sentences makes them contingent. There are various ways of coping with these difficulties, but it is not obvious that a *pure* disquotationalism remains intact.[6] Another important objection to disquotationalism is that the schema (DS*) does not account for a central feature of language, the compositionality of meanings: complex sentences are formed out of simpler ones, which determine their truth conditions. " Snow is white or grass is green" is true iff "snow is white" is true or "grass is green" is true, and in turn both these simpler sentences can be disquoted, but it does not account for the complexity of the sentence and for the way meaning is determined from truth conditions.[7]

2.3 Tarski's semantic theory
Up to now, we have not paid attention to the fact that although "true" seems to function quite well in natural languages as a device

of assertion, certain uses of it lead to paradox. This is well-known from the famous Liar paradox and sentences such as "I am lying" or

(1) This sentence is false

But if we apply the disquotational schema (D) to (1), we easily reach a contradiction:

(1′) "This sentence is false" is true iff this sentence is false

The same difficulty affects the redundancy theory and its variants, for if "true" disappears from our language, we are unable to express such semantic paradoxes. Deflationists might here say that these are exceptional uses of "true" that they do not need to consider; but since these paradoxes are supposed to pose a problem for the notion of truth, this relaxed attitude is displaced.

Concern for the Liar paradox is one of the chief motivations for what is perhaps the most influential deflationist conception of truth in contemporary logic and philosophy, namely Tarski's *semantic* conception of truth (Tarski 1930, 1944). On the face of it, it looks like a version of the disquotational theory, for Tarski takes truth to be a predicate of sentences within a language L that can be defined by using the (DS) schema, formulated as a "material adequacy condition":

(T) "S" (in L) is true iff *p*

which Tarski calls "Convention T", and where "S" is an arbitrary sentence of an *object-language*, and *p* a sentence of a *metalanguage* in which truth-for-L is defined. Tarski shows that by using the recursive structure of the sentences of L (the way they are constructed from their parts in a systematic way, through which the compositionality feature evoked at the end of the previous section is taken into account) one can define truth implicitly as conforming to a set of axioms of the form (T), or explicitly by reducing it to the primitive notions of reference and satisfaction, by using the resources of quantificational logic.[8] A *theory* of truth in the formal sense is then a set of axioms from which one can derive a set of theorems of the form (T). (This technical sense should not be confused with the non-technical sense introduced in §1.1 above). Given the object-language/metalanguage distinction, the semantic paradoxes are avoided, since the truth predicate can never be applied to a language *within* this language (so there is an open-ended hierarchy of metalanguages).[9] Because this construction needs the resources of logic and set theory and because natural languages give rise to semantic paradoxes, it cannot, according to Tarski, be applied to natural languages, but only to formal ones. This seriously limits its scope, for the "definitions" in question are only relative to particular languages, and merely partial.[10] So this can hardly be called a general *definition* of the concept of truth. All that it says is that for any sentence in a language, say "The cat is on the mat", truth is a property that characterizes "The cat is on the mat" if and only if the cat is on the mat. Another difficulty is that, as with what happens with the disquotational theory, the (T) schema presupposes the notion of translation or of propositional meaning, for the sentence on the right is supposed to be the translation of the one on the left, or to apply when the metalanguage is one that we understand to be the same sentence as the left-hand side. In spite of these limitations, Tarski himself sometimes presents his semantic view as a distinctive theory of truth in the philosophical sense, but in a deflationary mood, suggesting that it lays down to rest our more ambitious attempts at defining truth in a substantial sense.[11]

This "neutrality" of Tarski's conception has attracted a lot of positivists writers, such as Ayer, who took it as a tool in their antimetaphysical crusades. But it has also attracted philosophers who had no such deflationary commitments. For instance Popper (1972: Ch. 9) considers that the (T) schema expresses what is distinctive of a realist conception of truth ("The cat is on the mat" is true iff the cat *is* on the mat: the latter sentence cannot function if it does not report a fact). And a number of philosophers, especially Davidson (1984), have suggested that a Tarski-type implicit definition of truth can, in spite of Tarski's restrictions, be applied, with appropriate changes, to natural languages as well, and serve as a basis for giving an account of *meaning* in terms of truth conditions. The point is not that a *theory* of truth (in the formal sense) *is* a theory of meaning (a theory specifying the senses of all the sentences of a natural language), but that it can, in appropriate conditions, *serve as* a theory of meaning. Here, although Tarski's theory is not to be identified with the disquotational theory, we again encounter the difficulties of the latter.[12] Davidson is not a disquotationalist, for he does not hope to define truth completely using Tarski's resources. But he claims that on the basis of a very thin characterization of truth as a property of linguistic utterances that speakers are able to discern, we can build a "theory of meaning" for their language that will take truth to be implicitly defined. Unlike in Tarski's T-sentences, this does not presuppose the notion of translation or meaning, but Davidson has to provide, through a conception of the interpretation of utterances in a natural language, the appropriate conditions for this construction. Although he does not want to presuppose meanings or propositions, he is led to claim that the notions of translation, meaning, belief, interpretation and truth are interdefinable, and that there is no hope of "defining" truth in more primitive terms. So the overall theory does in the end give a "content" to the notion of truth (Davidson 1990).

2.4 Horwich's deflationist minimalism

A deflationist conception of truth thus cannot avoid two commitments: it takes truth to apply to the contents of thoughts, or to statements or propositions, and it takes "true" to be a genuine predicate of assertions, expressing a property, albeit not a substantive, but a merely "formal" or "logical" one. We could, in this respect, compare its status with that of the operator of conjunction "and" in ordinary logic. Once we have said that it stands for a certain logical function allowing us to conjoin two propositions and that produces true propositions when both conjuncts are true, there is not much more to be said about it.[13] Horwich's (1990) version of deflationism – which he calls "minimalism" – undertakes these commitments. He proposes that we construe the equivalence (E) thus:

(P) The proposition that p is true iff p

and take it as an axiom-schema from which we can derive an infinity of appropriate axioms for each potential sentence of English, although our understanding of "true" does not consist in a grasp of this infinity of axioms, but in the grasp of those that we can formulate. Since truth applies to propositions, there is no bar to translation. Horwich claims that (P) accounts for all the features of truth as a predicate (although he does not consider semantic paradoxes). Moreover, it allows us to express all the ordinary intuitions that we associate with truth. For instance nothing is lost of our "realist" intuitions if we take (P) to mean, alternatively:

(P1)   The proposition that p is true iff p corresponds to the facts

(P2)   The proposition that p is true iff things are the way it says they are

(P3)   The proposition that p is true because p

These are mere platitudes that do not, according to Horwich, add anything to (P). But this claim may seem surprising. For instance if we say, as an instance of the third platitude:

"Snow is white" is true *because* snow is white

aren't we saying something quite substantive, namely that the proposition that snow is white is *explained* by the fact that snow is white? But Horwich tells us that this does not detract from his minimalism

> In mapping out the relations of explanatory dependence between phenomena, we naturally and properly grant ultimate explanatory priority to such things as basic laws and the initial conditions of the universe. From these facts we deduce, and thereby explain, why for example
>
> Snow is white
>
> And only then, given the minimal theory, do we deduce, and thereby explain why
>
> "Snow is white" is true   (Horwich 1990: 111)

The fact that snow is white is explained by whatever explains it. This has nothing to do, according to Horwich, with our appending to it the predicate "true". Hence, he concludes, it has no *explanatory role* and it points to no "hidden essence" of truth. The same strategy can go through with the other platitudes. They are, in Blackburn's phrase, mere "Pentagon" ways of talking – idle paraphrases or mere conventional stipulations that cut no metaphysical ice (Blackburn 1985: 225). This, of course, is the gist of a deflationary conception: no more substantive property is needed.

Horwich's view is not, however, without difficulties. In (P) the sentence "p" appears twice, but in contexts that are distinct. In the first occurrence, it functions as a singular term replaceable by sentence *tokens*, that is, particular instances of English sentences-types (for instance, "It's hot" said by me on 1 August is a token of a sentence-type that could be uttered on many other occasions). But these tokens, assuming that they are given uniform interpretations, express propositions. In the second occurrence, a particular sentence is used. So Horwich's semantic apparatus is a sort of hybrid between the disquotationalist view and the commitment to propositions. Now, this commitment implies that we can make truth-claims only for sentences that we understand. So this assumes the notion of meaning. As Dummett has remarked,[14] no deflationary conception of truth that assumes the notion of proposition can avail itself of an explanation of meaning in terms of *truth conditions*, if these are constructed in a purely disquotational way: "'Snow is white' is true iff snow is white" is correct only if we know what "snow is white" *means*. So, if deflationism is correct, truth cannot serve to elucidate meaning, but rather it is meaning that has to be presupposed in order to elucidate truth. We need an independent account of meaning. It seems also that we need an independent account of *belief*, or *judgement* if meanings are the contents of our beliefs. Ramsey was in fact perfectly aware of this. For although he says, proposing his version of the redundancy theory, that there is "no separate problem of truth", he immediately adds: "The problem is not as to the nature of truth and falsehood, but as to the nature of judgement or assertion" (Ramsey [1930] 1990: 39). And, as we have seen above (§1.5), Ramsey had an account of the content of beliefs in terms of utility-conditions. So it would seem that what we need in fact is an *inflationist* (substantive) conception of meaning and belief in order to secure deflationist truth. Horwich is aware of this, and he argues that we can, on the basis of a deflationary theory of truth, defend a deflationary theory of *meaning* as well (Horwich 1998a).[15] He claims, in a Wittgensteinian vein, that all we need to account for meaning is a theory of the *use* of expressions. "True" will not be an exception, so the meaning of this familiar word will be exhausted by its use. Hence we have to sever the link between meaning and truth conditions. But this is far from being an innocent commitment, for a proposition is, after all, an entity that is supposed to be the vehicle of *truth*.

A final difficulty that arises for a deflationary account of "true" has to do with the principle of bivalence and truth-value gaps. It is often said that deflationism cannot even formulate the principle of bivalence, for

(B)   Either p is true or p is false

will amount to the principle of excluded middle:

(EM) Either p or not p

which is distinct. Redundancy or disquotation here will erase this distinction.[16] But to this deflationists can answer that they can still use (B) in the deflationary sense that it is part of our linguistic practice. But can they account for failures of (B)? This question has already surfaced in the case of the Liar sentences: some sentences may not be susceptible of truth or falsity, they may fail to express propositions, or fail to have truth conditions. Such sentences will be neither true nor false, or the fact that they are *untrue* will not mean that they are false. So the principle of bivalence will not apply, and there will be "truth-value gaps". This might be so, it has been suggested, for Liar sentences, but also for sentences that contain vague predicates ("bald", "young", "heap", etc.), for performative utterances, or for ethical sentences on the view that they merely serve to express emotions or feelings. In such cases, the equivalence schema or the disquotational schema either do not apply ("'Close the door' is true iff close the door" makes no sense) or they yield untrue instances ("'I'm bald' is true iff I'm bald" will be neither true nor false). Deflationists can here say that they restrict the scope of their view to sentences that are *determinately* true or false, and distinguish falsity from *untruth*. I shall not here examine the way in which they could accommodate vagueness and other truth-value gaps. But if they make these distinctions, they owe us an account of *when* truth is determinate, and when it falls short of literal truth. In other words deflationists need to give a criterion of why certain sentences are *apt* for truth, and why others can fail to be. We shall come back to this point below (§3.3).

2.5 The false modesty of deflationism

If we step back and abstract from its various versions, we can see that deflationism, far from being the modest-sounding conception of truth that it claims to be, has quite important negative implications. Since truth is a quite trivial or superficial property – a mere *quasi-property*, one could say – every hope of saying more than (E) or (D) is vain. As Ramsey (1990: 38) famously said, "there is no separate problem of truth, but only a linguistic muddle". To go further would be to try to lift oneself off the ground by pulling one's hair, like the Baron of Münchhausen. The deflationist's move can be called, after Blackburn, "Ramsey's ladder". The ladder takes us from a sentence at the bottom level, "*p*", to "It is true that *p*", to "it is a fact that *p*", to "it is *really* a fact that *p*", and so on, without any loss when one climbs the ascending steps: in fact the ladder does not make us move higher up, it is horizontal (Blackburn 1998a: 78, 294). And this applies not only to ordinary empirical truths, but also to moral, mathematical, aesthetic, metaphysical truths, and so on. Thus to move from "Torture is wrong" to "It is true (really true, morally true) that torture is wrong" would not add anything. Claims about theoretical entities in science, such as "There are electrons", would deserve the same treatment: it does not add to it to say that "It is true that there are electrons", and so the question of the truth of theories becomes trivial. Even a Berkeleyan idealist can agree that "There are tables" is true if and only if there are tables. This seems to rob talk of truth in a particular domain of any substantial sense, and to deprive us of any hope of asking genuine *metatheoretical* questions in various regions of discourse. But such questions are those that occupy philosophers most of the time. Of course, it is not the first time that philosophers have used a point about the logical form (or the "grammar") of a certain expression to defuse what they take to be a philosophical illusion: Kant's claim that existence is not a predicate, Russell's claim that names are really disguised definite descriptions, or indeed many of Wittgenstein's "grammatical" analyses, are instances of this strategy. The deflationary conception of truth itself can be considered, in a sense, as an heir of the long scholastic tradition that calls terms such as *unum, verum* or *bonum* "transcendental terms", which transcend the Aristotelian categories, and which have no separate sense: they are the most general features of reality because they apply to anything whatsoever.[17] Although the scholastics took *verum* to be a property, there is an echo of this in the view that formal features of truth exhaust its nature.

In contemporary philosophy, there is no shortage of views of this kind. As I have already mentioned, the logical positivists welcomed Tarski's semantic theory as a tool for the liberation from metaphysics. Such accents, with a less scientist overtone, are also present in Wittgenstein. He often seems to endorse a redundantist conception like Ramsey's and his conception of philosophy as a purely descriptive discipline concerned with the grammar of language, freeing ourselves from the illusions of metaphysics and the struggle to get outside language, harmonizes well with a kind of deflationism. For instance, in a well-known passage from the *Philosophical Investigations*, where he obviously comments on his previous views in the *Tractatus*:

> At bottom giving "this is how things are" as the general form of propositions is the same as giving the definition: a proposition is whatever can be true or false. For instead of "This is how things are", I could have said "this is true" (or again "this is false"). But we have
>
> '*p*' is true = *p*
> '*p*' is false = not-*p*
>
> And to say that a proposition is whatever can be true or false amounts to saying: we call something a proposition when in our language we apply the calculus of truth functions to it.
>
> (Wittgenstein 1958: §136)

Some contemporary philosophers, such as McDowell, have explicitly endorsed a form of deflationism about truth inspired by Wittgenstein's remarks, and defended what has been called "quietism", the view that deep metaphysical puzzles should be laid down to rest ("*Friede in der Gendanken*").[18] The deflation of truth thus paves the way for a deflationist attitude in many fields. Given the connections of this concept with those of proposition, meaning, reference, belief, logical entailment, justification, mental representation, concepts, and so on, this attitude will not leave untouched the philosophical accounts which, in contemporary philosophy, consist in attempting to analyse these notions in more substantive terms. In so far as these can be considered as *theoretical* enterprises, deflationism about truth leads us to suspect that Ramsey's ladder applies here too, for if such accounts are neither supposed to be true nor to reveal the essence of these central notions, what is their point?

Deflationism about truth pays a lot of dividends, but it has to pay the price, for it is not, as we have seen, without important philosophical commitments. Neither of them is uncontroversial. Moreover, it is not correct to say that it can account for all the usual properties of our use of "true". We can raise at least five main objections, in addition to those that have already surfaced before.

Take, first, the claim that truth is merely a "device" of assertion: to say that *p* is true is just to assert *p*. This sounds like a platitude, but it is not, for it means that the concept of truth has the same sense, or at least the same effect, as the concept of assertion. But it is dubious that, as a claim about the *meaning* of true, it is correct. As Bolzano remarked long ago, "It is true that *p*" and "*p*" do not mean the same thing.[19] The first is a claim about a property that a sentence or an assertion has, whereas the second is not. A partisan of the performative view could here say that "it is true" simply adds a mark of approval with no cognitive import. But we have seen that this does not account for all uses. So "true", although intimately tied to assertion, seems to register a different kind of commitment.

A second and related point is that to assert a certain statement one needs to believe what it says, or to understand it. Although there are, so to say, parroting uses of "true" (as when disciples hear from their guru that "Wisdom is square" and say "That's true" without understanding what the guru says), they are not normally taken as expressions of belief (but at most of half-belief, or of deferential belief after an authority).[20] To assert that *p* is also to have the intention of asserting it. But with the exception constituted by these deferential uses, the intention in question is an intention to express a belief, and in turn an intention of saying that a belief that one has is *true* (lying would not be possible otherwise). One cannot, in the same breath, make an assertion to the effect that one has a belief, and withdraw it at once. This is why, as Moore remarked, such utterances like "It rains but I believe that it does not rain", are paradoxical (and known as instances of "Moore's paradox"[21]). To assert that it rains is to imply, or to convey implicitly, that one believes that it rains; hence adding the claim that one believes that it does not rain leads to at least a pragmatic contradiction.[22] To this the deflationist could reply: to believe that it rains is to believe that it is true that it rains; hence to believe that it does not rain is to believe that it is false that it rains, and if to assert that it rains is to imply that one believes that it rains, hence that one believes that it is true that it rains, we reach the same contradiction. The redundancy of truth applies equally to belief, and the fact that we can get the same argument with belief as with assertion does not show that there is anything special about truth. Still, this shows that there is a special connection between belief and truth: belief, as it is often said, "aims at truth", in the sense that beliefs are the kind of mental states that have to be true for the mind to "fit" the world (whereas desires have the opposite "direction of fit": the world is suppose to fit our desires).[23] So, even if the preceding argument does not show that it *adds* anything to the notion of belief to say that these are states the contents of which are supposed to be *true* or *false*, this shows at least that we cannot dispense with this notion when we want to explain the nature of beliefs. These conceptual facts are all trivial, and the fact that we need, in order to explain the notion of belief, to appeal to the idea of a "fit" between mind and world shows that it is not easy to get rid of the correspondence intuition.

A third feature of our assertions and beliefs that a deflationist view is silent about is that they are generally made or held for certain *reasons*. To assert that p is to be prepared, in normal circumstances, to defend one's assertion and to give reasons for one's belief. In other words, it goes with the notion of belief (and with the notion of assertion in so far as asserting that p is to represent oneself as believing that p) that belief can, at least in principle, be *justified*. A mere account of "it's true" in terms of a mark of approval, as in the performative view, is not enough. So although, as we have seen, truth is not justification, the two concepts are intrinsically connected through the concept of belief. The deflationist might agree that this is true of the concept of *belief*, but that this does little to show that "true" and "justified" go together. But if, as we have seen with Horwich's minimalist version, deflationists admit that truth applies primarily to the contents of beliefs and of assertions in so far as we understand them, they have to grant this point.

A good way of bringing these three objections together it is to remark, with Dummett (1959), that a redundancy, and for that matter a deflationary, conception of truth in general does not account for the fact that truth is the *point* of assertion, or the goal that we are aiming at when we make assertions (and this is one of the senses in which beliefs "aim at truth"). Dummett compares assertion to a game: to omit the fact that it aims at truth is like omitting the fact that the purpose of playing a game is to win it.

But, fourthly, there is another important worry. We have already remarked, in connection with Horwich's theory, that it needs to take for granted the notions of propositions and meaning, and thus that it cannot avail itself of the possibility of explaining meaning in terms of truth. But there is a more radical consequence. When I say that it is true that George W. Bush is clever, I only say that George W. Bush is clever, or when I say that it is true that Italy is beautiful, I just say that Italy is beautiful. In each case these sentences mean different things (that *George W. Bush is clever* and that *Italy is beautiful*). Now, since "it is true" is, on the view considered, supposed not to add anything substantial to their meanings, and since these meanings differ, it follows that *in each case the word "true" means different things*. We can say that "true" has the *George-W-Bush-is-clever* meaning in one case, and the *Italy-is-beautiful* meaning in another, as if it were intrinsically attached respectively to these distinct meanings. But if this is the case, there will be as many truths as there are meanings to affirm, or as many truths are there are possible contents of assertion. Of course, one can say that there is a "core" (purely formal) meaning of "true" that is common to all, but since it does not contribute, according to deflationism, to the content of assertions, truth becomes radically relativized to meanings. But we certainly want to say sometimes that a sentence has a certain meaning, which is one thing, and that it is true, which is another thing. So the danger to which we are exposed, with a deflationist theory, is that of an extreme *pluralism*: not only does truth depend upon meaning, but it depends upon subject matter: certain true assertions are about cats, others about dogs, others about mathematical entities, moral entities, and so on. Each is relative to what it talks about. There are *truths*, but no truth. But we certainly often want to compare the status of truths in one domain (say science) to that of truths in another domain (say ethics, or fiction).[24] If truth were so radically pluralistic, these efforts would be pointless. We would just be happy to say that there is truth in astrology, in theology, in parapsychology, and all other pseudo-sciences. A perfectly *tolerant* and *relaxed* attitude!

The fifth and last objection is related to the previous one. It also bears upon the comparison between truths in a given domain and truths in another. According to certain philosophical views, certain kinds of talk, such as science, are literally true, in the sense of being about real entities in the world, and other kinds of talk, such as ethics or fiction, are about entities that are not so straightforwardly true, but only metaphorically so, or as a "way of talking". The view in meta-ethics known as *expressivism*, in particular, says that there are no moral truths in the usual sense, but that these are just ways of expressing one's feelings or attitudes. Now if truth is understood in the deflationary sense, as a mere device of assertion, there will be no difference between the "usual" sense and the more derivative one that such theories want to emphasize. For another example, take Bentham's (1959) theory of fictions. It is crucial for it that certain entities, such as natural rights, are merely fictitious ways of talking, and do not "really exist". If truth is merely a device of asser-tion, there will be no way to draw the appropriate contrast.[25] Of course, certain theorists want to annihilate the contrast, as in Derrida's view that every discourse is metaphorical, and that there is no difference between truth-talk and metaphor.[26] But they will be deprived of any possibility of saying that anything is metaphorical as well. This objection is a version of the one that we raised for the deflationary account of truth-value gaps. If some sentences fail to be literally true or to be *apt* for truth, the deflationist should give us an account of this.

2.6 Rorty, Nietzsche and Heidegger

The deflationists might just bite the bullet, agree that their theory has these consequences, and welcome them. One of the contemporary writers who has been quite consistent in this claim is Rorty. He approves the deflationary theory for freeing us from the metaphysical illusion that takes truth to mirror an independent reality that would make our statements true. He actually defends a version of the performative conception: truth is just a "compliment" that we pay to our assertions, a little "rhetorical pat" on their backs (Rorty 1982: xvii). There is no more to truth than the fact that we *accept* a number of our assertions. This is, according to Rorty, perfectly consistent with recognizing that the concepts of belief and truth are tied to the concepts of reason and justification. But we should not think of these in any absolute sense or in the sense of some objectively warranted or rational assertibility. For there are all sorts of reasons for which we might assert our statements and accept them as true: we like them, they are useful, they are shared by members of our community. These are "good" reasons, but there is nothing like a best reason, on which everyone would converge. We certainly value our truths, but Truth is not an ultimate goal of our enquiry. Rorty is also happy to acknowledge the pluralism of our ascriptions of truth. There is nothing in common – Truth – that various discourses, about science, ethics, politics, literary criticism, and so on would share. And it is, as we saw, a very relaxed and tolerant attitude towards all sorts of discourses. Let a million flowers bloom! This sounds like relativism, or subjectivism, like the Protagorean view that "Man is the measure of all things". But Rorty disclaims being a mere relativist. He prefers to call himself a "pragmatist". But his pragmatism is very different from the forms of this doctrine that we encountered above (§1.5): it is not the Jamesian sense in which truth would be defined as a form of utility, nor the Peircian sense of truth as the end of enquiry, but a merely negative sense: truth does not explain our relation to the world, and is supervenient upon the practical values and the conventions that we set for ourselves and upon our behaviour as natural beings in a natural world.[27] Such views, Rorty claims, are apt to promote the values of democracy and social solidarity, better than foundationalist moves in moral and political theory that emphasize the values of justice and truth. The immediate reaction that such views prompt is that they are not serious. For, to take up only the last point, it is not clear that democracy is better achieved by renouncing the ideals of truth and rationality. To this objection that he cannot *seriously* maintain such views (after all he is *promoting* them, and what is promoting if not promoting *as true*?), Rorty has answered that he is an "ironist", and that his deflationism should be taken in this mood. But this amounts to granting that it can hardly be a theory at all. As Ramsey would have said, it's not clear that he could whistle it either.

Much of Rorty's claims are based on a reading of the history of contemporary philosophy that is meant to imply that the metaphysical enterprises of philosophers of the past have been made vacuous by the naturalist outlook of twentieth-century philosophers like Dewey, Wittgenstein, Davidson, Quine and Sellars, among others, who are supposed to have helped us resist "the absolute conception of reality". It is not obvious, to say the least, that we can take his word for that. But among the immediate predecessors of his "pragmatism" he counts Nietzsche and Heidegger. So it could be interesting to compare their views with some of the claims that we have attributed to deflationism in general.

Nietzsche's writings actually contain many reflections on the nature of truth and on its value. According to his "perspectivism", we accept certain statements as true because we have certain values, which determine certain interpretations that we give to phenomena. But there is no objective reality beyond our interpretations and beyond the forces that drive them. Truth is essentially a matter of the will, of the will to power, and the transmutation of values implies that we move beyond the True and the False as well as beyond Good and Evil. It is important here to note that the Nietzschean strategy does not aim, unlike some positivistic and irrealist views, to eliminate the notion of truth – even though Nietzsche denounces metaphysics and truth as "errors" – but to provide an appropriate substitute for truth as value.[28] This substitute is itself a value, or a force, the will-to-power. Instead of the will-to-truth, we should put at the bottom of being and at the bottom of our inquiries a pure will as auto-affirmation. What is important, as Gilles Deleuze says, commenting upon Nietzsche, is not the true and the false, but the good and the bad (Deleuze 1962). In this sense, Nietzsche seems to be close to vulgar pragmatism, and when Deleuze tells us that "the notions of importance, necessity and interest are a thousand times more determinant than the notion of truth", it is not clear that the Nietzschean view goes farther than this. Deleuze however adds immediately: "I do not mean that they replace it [truth] but that they measure the truth of what I say" (Deleuze 1990: 117). If this is so, then a statement is true if and only if it is "measured by utility", and what else does it mean than that it is true because it is useful? But this claim, if it were Nietzschean, would clash with perspectivism, which says that no conception of truth has any prominence over the others (Shand 1994: 194). Nietzscheans are more consistent when they resist the temptation to defend any conception of truth whatsoever. Nevertheless it is also more in line with the will-to-power doctrine to take Nietzsche as an expressivist, in the sense above, about truth: truth is only a projection of our affects and feelings. The will-to-power which is being creates a flux of interpretations and there is "no truth" behind our interpretations.

There are thus strong affinities between (at least Rortyan) deflationism and Nietzscheism. It seems, however, harder to find affinities between it and Heidegger. For at first sight, Heidegger seems to side with the substantial or immodest conceptions, since he talks about the "essence of truth" as "disclosure" or "openness of the *Dasein* to Being", according to the etymology of the Greek word *alētheia,* which means revelation of what is hidden. This is closer to the conception of truth as a deep, Parmenidian, identity with Being. But Heidegger is also concerned to show that this conception is the typical *metaphysical* one, which he intends to bring out of his hermeneutical reading of Greek philosophy and its heritage in Western philosophy, and which is perpetually *brought to an end*. When he discloses the essence of truth, Heidegger again meets with Nietzsche's thought, by identifying truth with *will* and *freedom* (Heidegger 1931). But what has truth to do with freedom? By this Heidegger does not mean a mental event or an affirmation of the metaphysical doctrine of freedom of the will, but the fact that, through the disclosure of being, people "let being happen" (*sein-lassen*) as an event, which is the very disclosure of Being, and the very condition of possibility of truth as conformity to reality. Whatever that means, we are certainly very far here from the deflationist view that truth is just a simple, obvious concept reducible to the equivalence schema. But in his analysis of the structure of *Dasein* in *Being and Time*, Heidegger has emphasized the links between belief and action, and between what we believe about the world around us and the "utensility" of things as they are for us "ready to hand", or "available" (*Vorhandenheit*). Our most cognitive theoretical enterprises are thus made possible by the utility of our conceptions and their tractability within a familiar world. Truth is not utility, however, for this definition would belong to the reign of technical thought, which is the forgetfulness of Being. But the claim is there that there is no reality independent from *Dasein*, from our pre-understood practices. Truth as being can thus only be recovered *from within* these practices, in their utter banality. As Rorty has remarked, this sounds like his own "pragmatism", and he recruits it for his purposes (Rorty 1991).

If we understand it in a wide sense, it seems that the deflationary house contains many mansions. I do not want, however, to mount a case of guilt by association. I am not saying that the sophisticated attempts of analytic philosophers at constructing minimalist theories of truth automatically lead to the kind of nihilism and scepticism illustrated by Rorty on the contemporary scene and possibly by Nietzsche and Heidegger, nor that there is no difference between them. For in spite of the Grand Negative Claims made by the latter, which do not square so well with a *deflation* of philosophical ideals, there is a theoretical ambition in the former that is absent from the latter. But if we want to stick to this theoretical ideal, it is important to keep in mind these potential implications of deflationism.

3 Minimal realism

We have reached a sort of impasse. Our review of the various classical theories of truth has led us to suspect either that truth is indefinable or that there is no "substantive" definition of it, hence that only a deflationist account of truth can be given. But deflationism is inadequate and has unwelcome potential consequences. There is thus a tension between the fact that there does not seem to be *much* more to say about truth than what the equivalence or disquotational schema tell us, and the fact that these obviously do not tell us *enough* about the concept. But if we pull in the direction of the second intuition, shall we not be obliged to come back to some version of a substantive theory? To put it in Kantian terms, we have a sort of antinomy here, the *antinomy of minimalism*:

Thesis: truth is a more substantive concept than what deflationism says it is

Antithesis: truth is less substantive than what substantive theories (realist and anti-realist) say it is

The thesis seems to lead us to a reversal to a substantive position; the antithesis to a reversal to a deflationist position. Is there some stable middle ground? In philosophy, such intermediary positions (for instance, a form of non-reductive-materialism about the mind/body problem, or compatibilism about freedom and determinism) have proved hard to sustain, precisely because of the permanent pull in opposite directions. The view that I intend to put forward is not intermediary or conciliatory in this sense. It involves a strong commitment in favour of *realism*. But it also grants certain points to the minimalist programme about truth, and in this sense it falls somewhere in between the other views. This is why it deserves to be called *minimal realism*. This prompts an immediate objection: if, as Dummett has claimed, the question of realism itself depends upon some conception of truth,[1] a minimalist conception of truth cannot but affect these issues, and a deflationist view discourages any attempt to argue from a certain view of truth to realism or to anti-realism. So we shall have to part company with Dummett's claim, and to suggest an independent conception of the realism issue. But we shall also have to propose a form of minimalism that is *not* deflationist.

3.1 Wright's minimal anti-realism

Let us, then, try to put for the moment the question of realism to one side, and see whether a position that could restrict truth to a minimal concept without endorsing the troublesome implications of deflationism can be defined. The view defended by Crispin Wright in *Truth and Objectivity* (1992) seems to promise just that. He calls it a "minimalism" in the first place because it agrees with deflationism (in the disquotationalist or in Horwich's version, but not in the redundancy one) on the following points: (a) "true" is a predicate, (b) although a "lightweight" one; (c) it satisfies only formal or syntactic features: it obeys the equivalence or the disquotational schema, is such that statements that are apt for truth have negations that are likewise, is such that they can be embedded in conditional and propositional attitudes constructions; (d) it satisfies, in addition to the ones just mentioned, a number of characteristic "platitudes", which can be listed as in Box 1.

The list can be extended. I shall comment upon the last below.[2] All of these, including the one about correspondence, are platitudes, because, although they can lend themselves to more robust interpretations, they can be expressed as mere innocuous paraphrases of the disquotational property. For instance, that a true statement corresponds to the facts does not say more than that the statement represents the way things are, in the platitudinous or "Pentagon" sense. This much is common ground with deflationism.

Box 1: The truth platitudes
- To assert a statement is to present it as true (TRANSPARENCY)
- Truth-apt statements have negations, conjunctions, etc. (EMBEDDING)
- Truth is correspondence to the facts (CORRESPONDENCE)
- A statement may be justified without being true and vice versa (CONTRAST)
- Truth is absolute and has no degrees (ABSOLUTENESS)
- Truth is timeless (TIMELESSNESS)
- Truth is objective, and implies convergence (CONVERGENCE)

But Wright departs from deflationism when it involves the claim that "true" does not register any norm of assertoric discourse other than warranted assertibility. In other words, when deflationists say that "true" is merely a device of assertion, they deny that there is anything more to "it is true that p" than the mere assertion that p. As we have seen, deflationists are not obliged to adopt the performative theory according to which "true" has only an endorsing use. They can admit that it registers a reason, a justification or a warrant for the appended statement or sentence. That "true" involves such a claim can be called a *norm*, both descriptive and prescriptive, that characterizes our practice of assertion. But apart from this practice, "true" does not involve any other norm than this: people who assert a statement take themselves to be warranted in doing so. But, Wright argues, this clashes with our ordinary understanding of negation. We have already met this point in our discussion of verificationism (§1.4). It is put here in terms of the disquotational schema (DS) above (§2.2). Let "T" be a predicate (not necessarily "true") obeying this schema, and applied to the negation of "p":

(1) "not p" is T iff not p

This leads, by appropriate substitutions, to the "Negation Equivalence":

(2) "not p" is T iff not ("p" is T)

Now suppose "T" is warranted assertibility and apply it to (2):

(3) "not p" is T iff not ("p" is warrantedly assertible)

This fails from right to left, for the lack of warrant of "p" does not amount necessarily to the lack of warrant of "not p". When the states of information that are evidence for a statement justify neither it nor its negation, or are neutral, T cannot be warranted assertibility (Wright 1992: 20). So, concludes Wright, the T-predicate differs in extension from the predicate of warranted assertibility. Hence it must register a distinctive norm. Wright here takes up Dummett's point that deflationism does not account for the fact that, over and above being a device for assertion, truth is something we aim at (see the third objection in §2.5). But his rejection of the assimilation of truth with warranted assertibility leads him to part company with a purely epistemic or verificationist conception of truth. In this sense, says Wright, we cannot content ourselves with a deflated notion of truth, and we must "inflate", or enrich, the T-predicate so that it does not obey only the formal or syntactic features of disquotation, possibility of negation, conditional embedding, and so on, but must also obey *other* requirements. Now which ones? First, these are facts about the use of the words within a community, and in this sense facts about what they mean. For suppose that to say that "There is a cup here" is true could be cashed only in terms of the disquotational schema, hence equivalent to "There is a cup". For it to be an assertion that "there is a cup here" we have to make sure that the word "cup" is only used to refer to cups. Had it been used, say, to refer to mugs only, it would not have had the same truth conditions as "There is a cup".[3] So the facts about usage count, and this is just to repeat the point above (§2.4) that a purely deflationist-syntactic account must rely upon a theory of meaning and understanding of the contents of sentences. We have to take into account that our use of "p" when we equate it to "it is true that p" is normatively correct.

But, in the second place, we also have to take into account what counts as the correct use of "true" itself. And since we rejected the idea that there is no other norm than pure assertion or assent to sentences, there must be other norms. We have already articulated some of these in our objections to deflationism (§2.5); but one that is obvious is the *objectivity* or *intersubjectivity* of our truth claims.

It goes with our usual concept of truth that, in favourable circumstances, subjects are apt to *converge* on the claims that are deemed to be true, and that truth has, in this sense, a certain *stability*: a statement that is true is supposed, in some sense, not to be subject to immediate revision. This requirement of *convergence* or of community of judgement is a platitude too, and it can be added to our previous list as belonging to what David Wiggins has called the ordinary "marks of truth" (see Wiggins 1980, forthcoming).[4]

But is the convergence platitude so innocent? At this point, it seems, we have moved at one level above the mere conformity of the truth predicate to the discipline of syntax or of form. For if we suggest that there is a *best* way of converging upon the truth of a statement for a community of thinkers, we are led to the thought that truth is some form of ideal justification or verification, hence to an ideal epistemic state of conception. But we have seen its drawbacks, and its close alliance with the idea of correspondence at the limit, hence its commitment to a substantive conception. Wright, however, proposes here that there is a predicate, weaker than truth, but which can still serve as a T-predicate, by securing this stability and convergence features, the predicate of *superassertibility*. He defines it in the following way:

> (S) *A statement is superassertible if some actually accessible state of information – a state of information which this world, constituted as it is, would generate in a suitably receptive investigative subject – justifies its assertion and that will continue to do so no matter how enlarged upon or improved.* (Wright 1996a: 865)

In other words a statement is superassertible if it is warrantedly assertible and bound to remain so whatever information we could have to assert it or to refute it. There is some vagueness in this definition, for it is not clear what a "suitable" subject is, nor in what circumstances a statement would remain undefeated. But let us ignore this. The first conjunct of this definition explicitly ties superassertibility to assertibility; so it is an epistemic concept, relative to our information. Hence it does not satisfy the platitude that truth is not justification, and that our best justification might fall short of truth. But the second allows it to satisfy the convergence

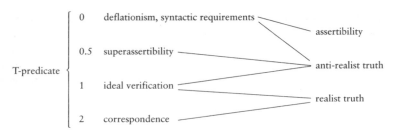

Figure 3

and stability requirement, *without* implying that the information is ideal or optimal. Wright claims that (S) passes the syntactic tests for being a T-predicate, and that it satisfies the negation equivalence (2) above, when (S) is put in place of (T). As we have just seen, superassertibility is not truth, and it is not ideal-limit assertibility either. So we could say it is situated at one level above the deflationist T-predicate and at one level below the ideal T-predicate, at an intermediary 0.5 level, as shown in Figure 3.

At this point, we might wonder whether superassertibility is at the service of an anti-realist, or essentially epistemic, view of truth or at the service of a realist, verification-transcendent one. But it is here that Wright dissociates his view from Dummett's. He claims that the issue of the nature of truth and the issue of realism are not systematically linked. A T-predicate, satisfying the syntactic and formal constraints, applies to a number of discourses. For instance it holds for ethical discourse. We can say that "It is true that 'torture is wrong'" is equivalent to "Torture is wrong", and make inferences from true premises to true conclusions, such as "Theft is wrong. This is a theft. Hence it is wrong." This, as we have seen, is the feature that most expressivist or emotivist views in ethics have difficulty in accounting for, for they are bound to say that moral sentences are not truth evaluable. Still it is not clear that such sentences are straightforwardly true or false in the strong realist sense, for we are in general not prepared to say that their evaluation is not beyond the reach of the best situated observers. This is even more so for talk about what is comic – where the property of being funny seems to depend *only* on our agreement – or for aesthetic judgements. But we may be prepared to have diverging – this time realist – intuitions in the case of empirical science, or mathematics. Nevertheless the mathematical intuitionists would disagree in the second case. In other words, a truth predicate may apply in various domains and satisfy the various platitudes. But it does not mean that we shall have the same story to tell about whether the features captured in each domain are *real*.

Wright suggests that the truth-predicate will not be uniform across all areas of our thought, and that the concept of truth can differ according to the local commitments made by different kinds of discourses. In some regions, these will favour a more anti-realist account, in some others a more realist one. So Wright is, apparently, committed to a *pluralism* about truth (§2.5) (Wright 1992: 141–2, 1996a: 905). There is a plurality of distinct predicates that can be candidates for truth, but not all of which will qualify as realist truth. We should be prepared, then, to accept that truth in some domains (ethics, mathematics) is essentially tied to verification and to epistemic constraints, although in other domains it is not. In this sense, Wright proposes that for ethics, superassertibility can be a "model" for truth. In all cases where truth is considered as *knowable in principle*, superassertibility will be enough. For instance, if mathematical anti-realism in Dummett's sense, or intuitionism, is correct, the truth-predicate will be superassertiblity.

Now it is open, in each case, to argue for a more realist or a more anti-realist view. The situation has been familiar since Plato's *Euthyphro*, which has become a paradigm for thinking about such issues.[5] Euthyphro sustains the view that

(a) Pious acts are such because they are loved by the gods

whereas Socrates argues that

(b) It is because some acts are pious that the gods love them

Now Euthyphro and Socrates both agree that

(c) An act is pious if and only if it is loved by the gods

But although this "basic equation" (c) characterizes a feature of piety on which all agree, it does not tell us more. The substantial disagreement is over whether it is (a) or (b) that is true. Euthyphro has an anti-realist view, and says that piety depends upon the judgements of the gods, whereas Socrates has a realist view, according to which it is of the nature of piety to attract the appreciation of the gods. This situation (the "Euthyphro contrast") is reproduced every time there is a potential conflict with a given concept between an account of it as depending upon the responses of subjects, or the best opinion, and an account that takes it to involve no such dependence. For instance, for colours we have the basic equation (or platitude):

(a)   Something is red if it would look red to normal observers under standard conditions

But the question whether colour depends essentially on the subjectivity of observers or whether colours are real features of objects (whether, as it is said, they "depend upon responses") has been a matter of dispute at least since seventeenth-century discussions of secondary and primary qualities. We could also draw a similar contrast for moral concepts, depending upon whether we have a more or less "response-dependent" account or a more realist one. The analogy with anti-realist/realist disputes should be obvious. The platitudes associated to the truth-predicate here play the role of the basic equations for piety or colour. They are mere touchstones for the truth aptitude of a given discourse. The question of whether one should be a realist or not in this discourse is a matter of whether one is prepared to say that truth here coincides with superassertibility or whether superassertibility can be explained further by some underlying trait. Wright suggests two criteria for recognizing that we might move in the second, realist, direction. The first is that we have some *cognitive command* of the domain. This means that when observers disagree on a feature of X, this can be traced to some shortcoming of their cognitive apparatus, because the feature is reliably tracked, in the usual cases, by this apparatus. A technical device, such as photography or tape recording, exhibits this, as well as sensory perception when it functions normally. The idea is that some reliable causal channel exists between reality and us, and that we can detect its failures. When cognitive command is in place, we have a clue to the reality of the feature in question. The second criterion is what Wright calls, somewhat pompously, *width of cosmological role*. It means that a subject matter can best be explained by independent states of affairs. A number of moral realists, for instance, accept this, whereas moral anti-realists or relativists reject it. When both this requirement and cognitive command are satisfied, the platitude that truth is correspondence to facts gets a more substantive meaning, and we have a recipe for holding a fully realist view in the domain.

What is distinctive of Wright's approach, then, is not only his *prima facie* pluralism about truth – which we have seen to be a potential implication of deflationism – but his pluralism with respect to the realist/anti-realist issues. When he takes truth to amount to the minimalist platitudes, he aims to give us a framework that is *neutral* between anti-realist and realist options, but this neutrality only lies at the surface, at the level where a truth-apt discourse can lend itself to the platitudes. When we dig further, either we can take talk of truth in the realist sense as a mere appearance, or we can take it at face value, and move to a causal realist explanation. This pluralism with respect to the realism/anti-realism issues is in fact quite alien to the deflationist perspective, since, as we have seen, the deflationist denies that these issues make any sense. On the contrary Wright, although he is prepared to empty the concept of truth from its purported substance, is not willing to consider the realism/anti-realism issues as empty. So his "minimalism", free of the deflationary implications, seems to be just what we need when we are looking for a position that would *both* accept the view that truth is a notion without much substance, and deny that it is merely a device of assertion and disquotation.

Still, Wright's minimalism is not itself without troublesome consequences. His pluralism about truth, the suggestion that "true" might not be a univocal concept, is one of them. I have spelled out the *prima facie* reasons for finding it problematic above (§2.5), but I shall leave it aside for the moment and come back to it later (§3.3). A second consequence of Wright's view that creates difficulties is his proposal that superassertibility can be, for a number of discourses, a "model" of truth. This raises two related questions. First, doesn't it have the effect that truth, if superassertability is a model of it, becomes essentially *epistemic*? In this sense Wright's view might well be called a form of *minimal anti-realism*. But if superassertiblity, as involving an epistemic conception of truth, can serve as a paradigm for truth *itself*, doesn't that clash with the claim, which Wright includes among his "platitudes", that truth is not justification or warranted assertibility? If we want to escape this consequence, we have to license the possibility of an epistemic conception of truth that would nevertheless be compatible with our realist intuitions (that truth is a matter of independence from knowledge, that it is about a world that is in causal contact with us, that is, just the features of "width of cosmological role" and of "cognitive command"). The notion of superassertibility is in fact just devised for filling this role. But it seems that it can fill it only if in some sense we reintroduce ideal verificationism, which is dubiously a view according to which truth might be independent from justification. The path of non-deflationist minimalism is very narrow.

The second question pertains to Wright's strategy, which he shares here with the deflationist. He puts forward some formal or syntactical features, together with associated platitudes, which by themselves assure that a predicate is a T-predicate, or that a domain where the T-predicate applies is "truth-apt". It is essential to this strategy that the T-predicate is *not* considered in advance to be the predicate "true", that is, that it is not the *truth*-predicate. This is why superassertibility, properly construed, can serve as a truth predicate without being truth itself. But we can raise here a question which has been advanced by David Wiggins (forthcoming). Call any predicate, say f, a T-predicate if, for every sentence S or any proposition expressible in a given language, we have: $f(S)$ iff S (where "(S)" is the name of a sentence in the language and the rightmost "S" is the sentence itself). The question then is: how can we fix the meaning of f without presupposing that it denotes *truth* itself? Why couldn't we say that truth is a model for superassertibility or for weaker notions rather than the contrary? In other words, it goes with deflationism and minimalism that we do not need to explain truth further than properly disciplined syntax and the ordinary platitudinous uses of "true". But these very features, according to Wright, can refer *both* to something that is truth *minus* more meaty commitments, and to a more substantive notion of truth. But how can we explain "true" as a mere syntactical device without presupposing that *truth* itself is a mere syntactical device? Moreover, what are Wright's "platitudes" associated with, if it is not with *our* ordinary concept of truth, and not with another concept? Correspondence, for instance, is not associated with superassertiblity. So the strategy of trying to define a neutral T-predicate seems to beg the question. At least, the way remains open for a more "inflated" concept of truth.

3.2 Putnam's "natural realism"

But how could we follow the preceding line of thought without coming back to a more substantive account of truth, that is, without being driven back to a substantive epistemic theory of truth or to a substantive correspondence realist view? This pendulum effect,[6] which is characteristic of the dialectical situation in these issues, is clearly present in its representation in Figure 3, where I have indicated a line leading from deflationism to anti-realism, and there is a line leading from ideal verification to realism, and where the intermediary position of superassertibility at level 0.5 between the null truth-concept of deflationism and the full-blooded realist notion or ideal verificationist notion at level 1 is a source of instability. It is also characteristic of the evolution of a thinker like Hilary Putnam. In the 1970s, Putnam defended a strong realist view of truth, based on a causal theory of reference and a form of correspondence conception. In the 1980s, he changed his mind, and, as we have seen (§1.2), repudiated the "absolute" conception of reality ("external realism") that his former view seemed to involve, and opted for a conception closer to ideal verificationism, which he called "internal realism": internal because truth can only be accessed within our investigative powers, realism because it was supposed to be about a real world, nevertheless independent from us. But aware of the limitations of an ideal verificationism, Putnam has defended, since the early 1990s, a view that he now prefers to call "natural realism", and which is supposed to avoid both the commitments of full-blooded external realism and of internal realism. Has he reached the stable resting position that we are looking for?

Putnam's starting point is very similar to the one that we took at the beginning of this chapter: "If we structure the debate in the way both Dummett and the deflationists do, then we are left with a forced choice between (a) either Dummettian anti-realism or deflationism about truth, or (b) a retreat to metaphysical realism"

(Putnam 1994: 498). Dummettian anti-realism, he argues, is wrong, because it transforms truth into an epistemic concept, and ties it to justification, thus rejecting our intuition that truth can transcend verification. But metaphysical realism is also wrong because it "feels compelled to appeal to something that *underlies* our language-games: a mysterious property that stands behind" (1994: 500). It is also wrong because it entertains the idea that true sentences *represent*, or fail to represent, this underlying reality. We have seen how Putnam discards this whole idea through his model-theoretic argument (§1.2), and he still does, although he is not prepared to put the same weight on this argument.

Now deflationism is wrong too, because it reacts to both the realist and the anti-realist pictures in thinking about the whole issue in the same terms. What the deflationist says in substance is that since only the representations, the sentences or the propositions that express them are there, and not any underlying property, there is no point to being realist or not. So the appropriate move, according to Putnam, is to reject the whole picture of a representation *of* something by whatever intermediaries one can think of: sentences, propositions, ideas, mental representations and events, sense data, and so on. This picture of an "interface" between us and reality is present *both* in classical idealism and empiricism *and* in contemporary materialist accounts of thought, which talk of "mental symbols" or of functional states standing in between the world and us. If we reject it, or "recoil" from it, Putnam suggests, we are led to the "common sense realism or the plain man", or the "naïve" view that what we perceive are the objects themselves, not some shadowy representations lying in between us and the world. Putnam here enjoins us to follow the lead of Aristotle, to whom the idea that perception is the perception of internal events was completely alien, of Aquinas, and of Austin, who, in *Sense and Sensibilia* (1962), rejected the whole sense datum conception of perception. The solution, therefore, consists in reverting to the problem of perception and to stop thinking, like most analytic philosophers, that knowledge of the external world comes primarily through intermediaries like sentences or judgements, and to espouse a theory of direct perception.

This, however, is only part of Putnam's story, for it does not tell us anything about truth as it applies to statements, sentences and judgements. The other part of the story is quite simple. Take, Putnam tells us, the sentence "Lizzie Borden killed her parents with an axe." We understand it, according to him, as true in the "recognition-transcendent" sense, simply when we understand that . . . Lizzie Borden killed her parents with an axe.

> How, then, do we understand "recognition transcendent" uses of the word "true", as, for example, when we say that the sentence "Lizzie Borden killed her parents with an axe" may well be true even though we may never be able to establish for certain that it is? . . . If we accept it that understanding the sentence "Lizzie Borden killed her parents with an axe" is not simply a matter of being able to recognize a verification in our own experience – accept it, that is, that we are able to conceive of how things that we cannot verify *were* – then it should not appear as "magical" or "mysterious" that we can understand the claim that that sentence is *true*. What makes it true, if it is, is simply that Lizzie Borden killed her parents with an axe. The recognition transcendence of truth comes, in this case, to no more than the "recognition transcendence" of some killings. And did we ever think that all killers can be recognised as such? Or that the belief that there are certain determinate individuals who are or were killers and who cannot be detected as such by us is a belief in magical powers of the mind?
>
> (Putnam 1994: 510–11)

The key to our problems, then, is simply to read Tarski's disquotational schema in the most straightforward realistic sense, but *without* entertaining the mysterious idea of correspondence.

But this "natural" reading does not seem to be very different from what deflationists and minimalists call the correspondence platitude. Putnam disclaims here siding with the deflationists, but he is very close to them. For he undertakes two commitments that we have seen to be characteristic of deflationism. The first is pluralism about truth. We should not, says Putnam, consider that there is, for each sort of discourse, a "free-standing property"; the rightness or the wrongness of our claims will vary in each case according to the subject matter. We have seen why: this is because truth claims can only be evaluated if we know what they mean. In turn, our understanding of what they mean will determine how we can take them as right or wrong. A proper deflationism must avail itself of a certain conception of the meaning, or of the use, of the sentences that lend themselves to our evaluations as true or false. This is why Horwich had to formulate his own deflationism in terms of propositions that we understand. Now Putnam makes exactly the same move: "Our understanding of what truth comes to, in any particular case (and it can come to very different things) is given by our understanding of the proposition, and that is dependent on the mastery of the 'language game'" (1994: 513). In other words, Putnam's "natural realism", in so far as it is a doctrine about truth, amounts to the view that our sentences are true because they correspond to reality. But "correspondence" here is a mere platitude. It can only be spelled out through the *use* of the sentence and our understanding of the proposition that it expresses. As Putnam says commenting upon Wittgenstein, "Wittgenstein says that 'This chair is blue' . . . corresponds to reality, but he can only say that by using the sentence itself" (1994: 513 fn).

So it is not clear that such a "natural realism" has made any step beyond deflationism. We could as well call natural realism *deflated realism*. As the quotations from Wittgenstein and the talk of "language-games" make clear, Putnam intends to take his inspiration for natural realism from Wittgenstein. I have already quoted in §2.5 the famous passage from *Investigations* §136, where Wittgenstein seems to endorse a deflationism about truth. Putnam, however, claims that Wittgenstein is here better understood as a common-sense realist, disdainful of all metaphysical attempts to settle the issue of realism itself.[7] But if our "realism" here and "our understanding of what truth comes to" depend upon our mastery of "the language-games", of *our* uses and practices, in their diversity and in their plurality, how can we say that what we understand is truth in the "recognition-transcendent sense"? For there is no external point of view from which we could evaluate the truth of our language-games. We are bound to use "true" *from within* our practices. But is that so different from Putnam's earlier internal realism, which rested on the denial that we have "a notion of truth that totally *outruns* the possibility of justification?"[8] And if it is not, in what sense does it differ from deflationism or from the sort of view that McDowell expresses, also commenting upon Wittgenstein:

[Wittgenstein says] "When we say, and *mean*, that such and such is the case – we and our meaning – do not stop anywhere short of the fact; but we mean: *this-is-so*." ... We can formulate the point in a style Wittgenstein would have been uncomfortable with: that there is no ontological gap between the sort of thing that one can think, and the sort of thing that can be the case ... When one thinks truly, what one thinks *is* what is the case ... But to say that there is no gap between thought, as such, and the world is just to dress up a truism in high flown language. All the point comes to is that one can think, for instance, *that spring has begun*, and that that very same thing, *that spring has begun*, can be the case. This is truism and it cannot embody anything contentious, like slighting the independence of reality.   (McDowell 1994: 27)[9]

Like Putnam, McDowell is in search of a form of "realism" that would "recoil" from correspondence and from the idea of an interface ("a gap") between thought and reality. But if the proper way to express it is to have recourse to a "truism", there is not much difference between this and deflationism, except perhaps that where deflationists reject metaphysical questions, quietists just shrug their shoulders.

There is, however, in natural realism, as Putnam describes it, a genuine commitment that goes beyond the mere platitudes about truth. It is the rejection of the interface conception, the "direct realism" that Putnam now favours. But it falls short of being "commonsensical" or "natural", for it is an elaborate epistemological thesis about the nature of knowledge and perception that is far from evident. On the one hand, it is not obvious that all forms of views that have been called "direct realism" in the history of philosophy are free from the interface image. For instance Thomas Reid, who is often considered to have held such a view, took sensations to be internal "signs" of real objects.[10] On the other hand, other forms of direct realism for perception that do try to get rid of intermediary representations as "interface" between the processes of perception and the environment are far from "naïve".[11] Direct realism in the philosophy of perception is not a self-evident thesis. It needs, for instance, a lot of argument to cope with such problems as that of hallucinations. And it also needs to answer a traditional objection that has been present at least since the seventeenth century from the time when what Sellars calls "the manifest image" of reality has been contrasted with "the scientific image". The objection is articulated in a well-known observation by Russell in his *Inquiry into Meaning and Truth*:

> We all start from "naïve realism", *i.e* the doctrine that things are what they seem. We think that grass is green, that stones are hard, and snow is cold. But physics assures us that the greenness of grass, the hardness of stones, and the coldness of snow, are not the greenness, hardness and coldness that we know in our experience, but something very different . . . Naïve realism leads to physics, and physics, if true, shows that naïve realism is false. Therefore naïve realism, if true, is false, therefore it is false. (Russell 1944: 13)

To resist such a line of argument, as Putnam is aware, and to maintain that the naïve realist picture, according to which we perceive objects directly, implies an appropriate response to the kind of scepticism that is bound to arise with the interface image: if what we perceive are representations, sense data, and so on, how can we be sure that what we perceive are real objects and that we *know* them? Here the theory of truth is not enough. It must, if it is to vindicate our realist intuitions, depend upon the theory of knowledge, and what is needed for naïve realism is an appropriate realist theory of knowledge.

Although Putnam sometimes talks as if a naïve theory of knowledge and perception were just as "natural" as the corresponding naïve realist theory of truth, it is not. Knowledge implies truth: to know that p implies the truth of p. But even if knowledge is thus partly defined in terms of truth – truth is a necessary condition for knowledge – a mere deflationist conception of it will not provide a definition of knowledge, for we also need a sufficient condition for knowledge itself: the mere truth of p, when we believe p, does not entail knowledge of p, for one might accidentally hit on the truth of p without knowing it, as has been familiar since Plato's *Theaetetus*, and from contemporary discussions of Gettier's problem (Gettier 1963). One way or another, we shall need an account of what makes knowledge *knowledge*. But at this point, if "natural realism" about truth accepts, as we have seen, the verification transcendence of truth, that is, the idea that our best theories might well be *false*, hence only *contingently* true, it is difficult to say this without taking these theories as a mere interface – in the bad cases a false one – between us and reality. In other words, when what we pretend to know is not *really* known, the "not really" seems to be justified only by the failure of our theories to correspond to "the facts". And thus we come back, willy-nilly, to the interface picture. If we do not want to entertain it, there seems to be no choice but to give criteria by which our beliefs and theories could be reliable, justifiable, warranted, and so on. We have to say what is the best evidence for our beliefs, and in what conditions. This is the object of a theory of knowledge. But if we embark on this enquiry, how can we avoid giving the optimal criteria of epistemic warrant, hence the criteria of our best ideal theory? In this sense, it is unclear that the proper formulation of ideal verificationism has to be completely abandoned. We can avoid it only by coming back to metaphysical external realism, by saying that it is in the *nature* of our states of mind to track an independent reality. But this picture, Putnam tells us, eludes us. So here again we reach the conclusion that we have not escaped the alternative between "internal realism" (or ideal verificationism) and metaphysical realism.[12]

3.3 Truth and truth-aptness

The difficulties of Putnam's position show that realism doesn't come cheaply, but they also raise problems for one line of thought that emerged from Wright's minimalist position, as well as, potentially, from deflationism. It is the *pluralism* about truth that seems to go with the idea that although a number of discourses are candidates for being true or false – or being "truth-apt" – it is a further matter to see what *kind* of truth we are dealing with in each case. Pluralism accepts that we take a number of discourses as truth-evaluable *at face value*, including those where the issue is problematic – namely all the discourses, such as ethics or comedy, where the properties referred to seem to depend upon our responses, feelings, and so on – but it postpones as a *further* issue the question of whether a more robust conception of truth, either of the realist or of the anti-realist kind, is correct for each domain. So in one sense, at the surface so to speak, there is "no problem about truth" in each case; but in another sense the problem of the nature of truth within each domain is left open. This leads to the idea that there might be different conceptions of truth appropriate for each domain, depending on what side of the *Euthyphro* contrast one sides with. But, as we have already noted at the end of §3.1, there is a potential incoherence here. For on the one hand, if the criterion of truth-aptness is just the capacity of a predicate for each domain to behave "syntactically" or formally as a truth-predicate, then in this sense all discourses are equal, and truth-aptness is a well-shared property. And if, on the other hand, it is a further issue that can only be settled locally, how can it make for different "kinds of truths" in each respective domain? For if the different kinds are kinds of *truths*, how can *truth* be thought of as uniform in the first place?

The problem, as we have already noted (the last objection in §2.5), arises in particular for domains where we want to hold that the correct account of truth-aptness is distinct from the surface account, in particular in ethics. Expressivism in ethics says that ordinary moral judgements such as "torture is wrong" are *not* truth-apt: they are neither true nor false, but are expressions of feelings or emotions. But, on the minimalist picture, if truth-aptness amounts just to "syntactic discipline", the expressivist view is automatically ruled out. This can be seen easily if truth-aptness is just a matter of satisfaction of the disquotational schema. The preceding judgement is truth-apt just if:

"Torture is wrong " is true iff torture is wrong.

But this begs the question, since the problem is precisely whether the right-hand side of this biconditional *is* truth-apt. The expressivist denies this. The argument has been precisely formulated by Paul Boghossian (1990). A deflationist about truth-aptness has to say:

(a) The predicate "has truth condition p" does not refer to a property

and has to say, about any sentence S:

(b) "S has truth conditions p" is not truth conditional

But (b) entails

(c)   "true" does not refer to a property

For the truth value of a sentence is fully determined by its truth conditions, which are presumably determined by the facts the sentence is about, or the objects and properties it denotes. But (b), when it denies that "S has a truth condition", has itself truth conditions, hence presupposes that it is obvious why it is so: it supposes that we have a criterion for distinguishing the sentences that are truth-apt from those that are not. If, for instance, an ethical statement lacks a truth condition, we must be able to say that other kinds of sentences do not lack truth conditions. And this presupposes a robust conception of truth. Hence (b) contradicts (c) (Boghossian 1990: 175; Wright 1992: 232). The argument applies readily to a redundantist or performative conception. But a deflationist *à la* Horwich, or a minimalist *à la* Wright, and probably a natural realist *à la* Putnam, deny that the disquotational schema is enough. Their view is that minimalism has to be *disciplined* in order to account for the norms of assertion. They say that we have to understand the *proposition* expressed by "Torture is wrong", and the *correct* use of this sentence in a declarative sense in our moral discourse as governed by certain norms of assertion. So a sensible deflationist or a minimalist does not accept (a). Horwich, for one, does not deny that truth is a property, although he maintains that it is not a substantive one. Boghossian's argument does not work either against Wright's minimal anti-realism, which says that truth can be modelled by superassertility, and *is* a property even in this etiolated or weak sense. The best we can have, if one is a minimalist about truth-aptness, is another argument:

(a′)   The predicate "has truth condition p" does not refer to a
       substantive property

(b′)   "S has truth conditions p" is not truth conditional

(c′)   "true" does not refer to a substantive property

which is valid if "truth conditional" is understood in the weak sense. But the question is left open whether "truth conditional" really refs to a non-substantive property. Disciplined minimalists about truth-aptness say that the answer is positive. So, for ethical truths, for instance, they move to the same conclusion as deflationists about ethical truth: *we do* understand it that way, it satisfies the usual platitudes, hence ethical discourse is truth-apt, so expressivism is threatened. But this transfers the problem only one step further, for an expressivist can still insist that for all that, "Torture is wrong" is neither true nor false, because it does not have truth conditions. Jackson *et al.* (1994), who put forward this objection, remark that in general there is an analytical tie between truth-aptness and *belief*: a sentence that is truth-apt must be used to give the content of a belief (see the second objection in §2.5). It is not enough to say that to believe that *p* is to believe that *p* is true. Hence we need an independent theory of belief.[13] But an expressivist can deny that sentences like "Torture is wrong" express beliefs. Hence the problem is still with us. It should not be solved so easily. There are in fact two issues: one is whether *truth* is minimal, the other is whether *truth-aptness* is also minimal. It is not clear that this is the same question, for the first bears upon our *concept* of truth, and the other on the *property* of truth. A positive answer to the second is not provided by a positive answer to the first. This can also be seen from areas where we are not tempted into giving an expressivist answer to the question of truth-aptness. For instance, a realist about theoretical entities in science might agree that "There are electrons" is true if and only if there are electrons. But the issue of realism in this area will not be solved by this observation. Scientific realists certainly want to say here that such sentences are truth-apt. But they must tell a further story over and above this simple equivalence.

The deflationist or the minimalist could retort here: but on what grounds do we say that truth and truth-aptness may diverge if not upon the ground that truth-aptitude holds in virtue of some underlying *fact* – or some underlying non-fact? Wright objects to Boghossian's argument that it presupposes that there is a well-understood distinction between the discourses that are objective (or that are in the business of describing reality) and the discourses that are not (which are merely expressive) (Wright 1992: 231–6). In other words, is objectivity itself objective?[14] Minimalism about truth-aptness does not assume this. But precisely the point is that *this* minimalism is not evident. Wright and Putnam certainly accept this point, since Wright grants that we may be more or less realists in various areas, and asks whether a discourse satisfies not only the usual platitudes, but also more substantive marks such as cognitive command and width of cosmological role,[15] and Putnam that a theory of direct perception must back natural realism. But this shows that there must be something wrong with their pluralism about *truth*: for what are these marks if not marks of truth-*aptness*?

The idea that "true" might be an ambiguous word, which changes its meaning according to the various subject matters, is highly unintuitive. The predicate "exists" certainly applies to a lot of things: to tables, chairs and people, but also to mental states, to numbers, or to entities out of space and time. We can agree that it is a different thing for a table and for a number to exist, or, to speak in Wittgensteinian idiom, that the word "exists" has a different "grammar" in each case, and that it is often a philosophical mistake to think of the grammar as uniform across subject matter. But these are facts about the nature of the entities in question or, in less onto-logical terms, about our concepts of them. This does not license us to say that "exists" has a different meaning in each case. The same could be said about identity: identity is a relation of equivalence, everywhere characterized by symmetry, reflexivity, transitivity and congruence of properties (by Leibniz's law of the substitutivity of identicals and by the principle of the indiscernability of identicals and its converse) but which is constituted differently whether it applies to material objects, persons, or abstract entities. Similarly for "true". It is a different thing for "Torture is wrong" to be true, than for "There are electrons" or for "Groucho Marx is funny." But that does not mean that "true" is ambiguous (see Sainsbury 1996). What we want to ask, in all such cases, is whether these are true *because* of underlying features, or whether these are neither true nor false *because* such features are missing. The truth-predicate is constant across the domains and it has the same role everywhere, but the way the property that it denotes is *realized* is distinct in each case. Wright agrees clearly with that, and accepts that "true" can be a univocal predicate, in the same sense as the sense in which "identical" is a univocal predicate identified by Leibniz's law and associated principles, although the criteria for A being identical with B can vary according to subject matter. So he can agree that his view should not be formulated in terms of a pluralism about truth, but rather in terms of a *functionalism* about "true", in analogy to functionalism in the philosophy of mind. Just as, according to functionalism about mental states, our use of "belief", "desire" and other mental terms can be individuated in terms of the role that they play, together with other states, in mediating between inputs and outputs, we could say that the predicate "true" is a place mark for a certain role marked by the usual platitudes: asserting statements that one believes, which correspond to reality, on which people can converge, and so on. But the issue of the nature of the properties that "realize" these roles is left open.[16] But to leave it open does not mean that it will be *always* left open. For this would bring us back to deflationism, for a deflationist will be quite happy to say that there is "nothing more" to truth than this function. What we have to say is that, just as for functionalism mental states as roles are second-order properties that have to be realized in various ways in first-order physical properties, truth is a second-order property of our statements, which has to be realized in various ways in first-order properties that will underlie this role. In each case we shall provide arguments to ascertain whether or not the realist story is correct.

As I just noted, to a large extent, this functionalist line of thought about truth can be accepted by a minimalist such as Wright (1996a: 924, 1998: 186). But he nevertheless tells us that "the general rule is that realism has to be earned" and that "antirealism is the default position" (1992: 149). His recipe is: start from the minimal platitudes, and assume an underlying anti-realist story, for which superassertiblity can play the appropriate functional role. As Timothy Williamson notes,

> Wright assumes that realism must by earned by philosophers in speaking *about* a discourse, because it must be earned by participants *within* the discourse. Unless they do something special to introduce realist content, their discourse will have only anti-realist content.   (Williamson 1996: 907)

But why should we follow Wright in this? Why not suppose that it is *realism* that is the default position, and that anti-realism has to be earned? The answer, of course, is that Wright considers that the verification-transcendent realist concept of truth is too weighty. But one might disagree: it may be the anti-realist, epistemic conception of truth that bears the heavier weight.

3.4 Minimal realism stated

It is now time to recap and to move on. We now have the main ingredients to try to canvass a view that is in the spirit of the previous attempts examined in this chapter to steer a way between the Scylla of a deflated conception of truth and the Charybdis of a too substantive conception, but that differs in important respects from these attempts. The need for such a view is certainly felt by many writers when they appreciate what I have called the antinomy of minimalism, but this feeling is not specific to the contemporary analytic philosophers whose theories I have been dealing with. In a sense, everyone wants to conciliate our basic intuitions about truth within a single theory that would (a) be sufficiently neutral to account for the fact that our use of the predicate "true" is pervasive in many discourses and justifiably so, (b) be compatible with the ordinary logical behaviour of this predicate, (c) be compatible with the basic platitudes that we associate with truth and with common sense, and (d) cut enough philosophical ice to be worth calling it a *theory*. The substantive metaphysical views of the past do not make exceptions. For instance, when scholastic philosophers said that "true" is a "transcendental term" (§2.5), they seemed to say something quite close to (a), although they certainly, like Aquinas, defended correspondence conceptions as satisfying feature (d). When philosophers such as Kant say that the traditional definition of truth as correspondence is just a "nominal definition", this can be understood as a desire to satisfy feature (c), whereas his account of the truth of judgements as a filling up of concepts by intuitions is an explanation of kind (d). Similarly we have seen that it is not easy for coherence theorists to keep their theory pure, and that they have to acknowledge some sense of truth as correspondence. This too can be understood as a response to the urge of not throwing away the basic intuitions.

One could think of the task of a theory of truth as providing what Rawls has called, in the domain of moral theory and for the concept of justice, a "reflective equilibrium" between our various intuitions and our higher-order epistemological or metaphysical principles. But here Frege's regress problem lurks. Such a method of reflective equilibrium is obviously coherentist and, as Rawls calls it, "constructivist": it tries to construct the best overall coherence between various intuitions and principles. But then truth itself would have to be some sort of coherence, if the theory produced is supposed to be *true*. And there is no reason to think that we could construct the concept of truth out of the consensus of a society in the way the concept of justice could be so constructed. So a sort of conciliation of the best views is not in order here.

I do not know whether my account is "conciliatory" or the product of the reflective equilibrium of various intuitions and principles. In many ways, it is not. The best I can do is to try to state the conception that I propose, and that I think has emerged from the foregoing discussion, which we can chart in Box 2. I call the conjunction of the set of theses (A) and of the set (B) *minimal realism* (MR).[17] I do not pretend that the label, nor the family of views to which this one belongs, are very original. William Alston (1996) has defended a similar view under this name (although he prefers "alethic realism"). Kraut's (1993) "robust deflationism", Johnston's (1993) and Michael Lynch's own views (1998) are also close to the one defended here.[18] In different ways, Robert Almeder's "blind realism" and Susan Haack's "innocent realism"[19] aim at capturing related ideas, and of course Putnam or Wright, in spite of the difficulties that I have pointed out for their views, are in this neighbourhood, although the kind of minimal realism that I intend to propose here is distinct.

In a number of respects, MR is meant to be a position quite akin to Wright's minimalism, although unlike him, I do not defend pluralism about truth, I distinguish truth from truth-aptness, and I take realism, and not anti-realism, as the default option on realism and anti-realism issues. I have remarked above that Wright's view might also be called a *minimal anti-realism*. I intend my view to be a sort of inverse mirror image of his. It is quite important to distinguish the minimalist part (1–4) of MR from its realist (5–7) part. The former does not say that the content of our usual truth ascriptions implies a reference to an independent and free-standing reality, apart from the platitudinous sense that true statements correspond to the facts, or that things are the way these statements say they are. In particular many of the authors just quoted tend to consider minimal realism to be just a version of the correspondence

---

Box 2: Minimal realism (MR)

A. Minimalism

1. MR agrees with minimalism on the fact that truth is a "thin" notion satisfying the discipline of syntax and the associated platitudes about assertion, correspondence, convergence, etc.
2. It rejects, however, the thesis that truth is a mere logical device of assertion or of disquotation; truth registers a distinctive norm.
3. It takes truth-bearers to be propositions, or the contents of beliefs, and assumes that we need to have an independent account of these contents.
4. It is not, however, pluralistic, since it does not take the truth-predicate to be ambiguous with respect to different domains; truth has a uniform core-meaning defined by its role (which is (1)), but which is realized in different ways from domain to domain.

B. Realism

5. The uniformity of the truth-predicate does not neutralize the issues about realism and anti-realism that arise from domain to domain; a minimalism about *truth* does not imply a minimalism about truth-*aptness*.
6. In each domain, truth-aptness is to be judged after the realist criterion of the independence of a domain from our responses, and of verification transcendence: our best conceptions might be false.
7. In each domain, realistic truth, in the sense of (6), is the norm of our enquiries.

---

platitude. For instance Lynch (1998: 126) formulates it thus:

(MR*)   *The proposition that p is true if, and only if, things are as the proposition that p says they are*[20]

But, as we have seen, this is something that a deflationist like Horwich, or a minimalist like Wright, can perfectly accept. So

(MR*) is *not* the version intended here. Similarly Alston's formulation of alethic realism (1996: 22) is something like:

(A) *A statement is true iff what the statement says to be the case is actually true*

The adverb "actually" is meant to capture the independence of the fact, or of the reality, described on the right-hand side. But again, it does not add anything; in this sense I agree with deflationists (remember Ramsey's ladder). Suppose we said that torture is wrong if and only if torture is *actually*, or *really* wrong. This would not change the status of this statement into a fact-making status. Moral statements lend themselves to truth talk, but it is a further matter whether they are actually true or false, that is, whether we are going to give an expressivist or a realist account of their truth-aptness. Alston, however, is closer to MR in my sense when he says "Though a particular realist or anti-realist metaphysical position . . . has implications for what propositions are true or false, they have no implications for what it is for a proposition to be true or false" (1996: 78).

Another point is that MR in my sense is not meant to be particularly "commonsensical" or "natural". Of course the talk of "platitudes" associated with the concept of truth is intended to capture most of the ordinary use of this concept. But I am not suggesting that common sense is uniformly realist about various subject matters, nor that, if it were so, we would have to follow it. Actually, in spite of the usual assumption that "the naïve realism of the common man" implies a commitment to a mind-independent reality that is there whatever we think or do about it, it is not obvious that common sense is realist through and through. For instance it may not be in the case of aesthetics matters, or matters of taste. It may not be realist in ethics either. Actually in many areas we might even say that common sense is relativist. As I remarked in the Introduction, many people, even those who are not sophisticated postmodernists, seem to accept without flinching some sort of Protagorean view that truth is a matter of opinion, that there is no such thing as scientific truth, and so on. Maybe common sense these days is not what it used to be! In any case one philosopher's common sense is often another philosopher's falsehood.[21]

Let us come now to the hardest part of a defence of MR. MR and positions of a similar kind are open to two kinds of objections, which reproduce the antinomy of minimalism above: the charge of triviality, of not saying much more than the platitudes (in which case MR is better conceived as a form of minimalism than as a form of realism); and the charge of reverting to a metaphysical realist view (in which case it is more a realism than a minimalism). But a satisfactory answer to the second charge will also give us an answer to the first, for if we can articulate a proper form of realism, it will have to be not trivial. So let us take the second horn of the dilemma first. The question is: how can it be that truth is just a minimal concept with no substantive implications and that realism is nevertheless said to be the *default* position for all discourses? Doesn't that imply a strong commitment to metaphysical realism and to a correspondence theory, especially since truth-aptness is taken to involve verification transcendence? In other words, doesn't the realist part of MR clash with its minimalist part? Such a threat of inflation of the notion of truth into a commitment to realism was not present in Wright's view, for his anti-realist "default option" harmonizes well with his minimalist view that truth is, at the surface level, just a matter of disciplined syntax, applied to entities that are either mind-dependent or language-dependent, namely sentences, propositions or statements. It was possible to say that realism had to be "earned" by adding to superassertibility stronger extra features. But in MR we do not take superassertibility as a model of truth: it is rather the recognition-transcendent concept that is our model.

To the suspicion that MR inflates too much the minimal concept of truth, we can answer that it is not clear that the proper approach is to take the settlement of a realist/anti-realist issue in one domain to be the *addition* of realist elements, when needed, to the minimal concept of truth, rather than *substracting* realist elements to move to an anti-realism in the domain. A complete justification of this claim can only be given by examining what happens in various domains where the realist/anti-realist issue (or the *Euthyphro* contrast) arises. I shall try to spell this out a little more in Chapter 4. For the moment, let us try to say why *realism* is better taken as the default option. My argument here, inspired by considerations put forward by Timothy Williamson, will rest upon some links between the concept of assertion and the concept of knowledge.

3.5 Minimal realism and the norm of knowledge

One point that emerged from my preliminary discussion of the difficulties of deflationism (§2.5) was that truth cannot simply be a device of assertion or disquotation, for there is an important conceptual connection between the concept of assertion on the one hand, and the concepts of belief, of justification and of warrant, on the other, which cannot be completely analysed in terms of assent to certain sentences. I have agreed with Wright's discussion of truth as registering a *norm* distinct from mere assertion. In this sense, it is essential for MR to defend thesis 7, that truth has a normative character. This will be the main topic of Chapter 5, but a general discussion of this point is needed here.

As it is often noted,[22] there is a weaker and a stronger sense of the notion of norm. In the weak sense a norm is simply a rule descriptive of a practice, for instance when we say that there are norms for politeness or car-driving. Norms, in this sense, are just conventions. This notion of norm does not bring with it some necessity or obligation to follow such norms: others might be more relevant, and sometimes it is better to follow other norms in our dealings with people (it is good to be polite, but that is certainly not enough). On the stronger notion of norm, a norm is not merely a description of a practice, but in some sense foundational and constitutive of it. The latitude in the choice of other norms is not really permitted. For instance, if equality is a norm of justice, it is essential to justice that it prescribes equality of treatment. Now we may conceive of truth as a norm in the first sense, as a rule simply describing our linguistic practice of assertion: what we do when we assert certain sentences is to assert them *as true*. But deflationists can be quite happy with that: it will not detract from their view if they use "norm" in this weak sense.[23] So when I say that truth is a norm, I intend it in the second stronger sense, that truth is *constitutive* of the practice of assertion, but also of judgement and of belief. This is what Wright, following Dummett, actually says: if we described the practice of a community who had a device of assertion without mentioning that assertions aim at truth, or if we described people as having beliefs without these aiming at truth, our description would be incomplete and inadequate (Wright 1996a: 909). But why should this point not lead us to accept Wright's form of minimal anti-realism?

I agree with Wright that truth is a norm in the strong sense; but I disagree with him on the *content* of this norm. Wright's picture implies that the content of this norm is a special form of warranted assertibility: superassertibility. A discourse obeys the norm of truth if it carries with it the requirements of syntactic discipline and if it aims at superassertibility as a model for truth. But the discourse does not need, on his view, to carry over to *realist* truth, although it can, if realism happens to be justified within a specific domain. On the contrary, MR implies that the norm of truth is the norm of *realist*, recognition-transcendent truth. In order to defend this thesis, we need to say more on the link between assertion, truth and warranted assertibility.

It is, as we saw, analytic (or constitutive) of the concept of assertion that assertions are supposed not only to be true, but also to be warranted, or justified by certain reasons. But it does not seem, *prima facie*, that it is analytic that assertions are warranted or justified for *conclusive* reasons. For otherwise to assert that p would amount to asserting *knowingly*, or with *full* justification, that p. When I assert that p, it does not seem to imply that I *know* that p, for p might be false, and of course we make (willingly or not) false assertions. One can assert that p for certain reasons, but these might fall short of being (objectively) *good* reasons. In other words, "assert" is not a "success" verb. Here the concept of assertion, or of linguistic assent, seems to be the counterpart of the concept of belief. The latter is often taken to be a sort of silent or private act parallel to linguistic assertion (a form of mental assent). "Belief", similarly, is not a success word: one can believe things that are false. But, on the most common analysis of knowledge, belief that p becomes knowledge when p is true and is fully justified, or conclusively so. This is the traditional analysis of knowledge as "justified true belief", and epistemologists are usually in the business of trying to spell out what this extra condition for full justification could be. Now, there is an obvious connection between this traditional analysis of knowledge and the analysis of warranted assertibility given by Wright. We might say that, for him, truth is a standard of warranted assertibility, but not of *fully justified* or conclusive warranted assertibility. This is what the notion of superassertibility is meant to capture: in appropriate conditions, we might reach undefeated and stable, but yet not completely conclusive, reasons. This is why Wright says that superassertibility is a good model for truth in all the domains where we can know something. Or, as he puts it, superassertibility is at least a necessary condition for knowledge:

(K) *If* p *is knowable, then* p *is superassertible*

Wright does not take the converse to be true in general: superassertibility is not a sufficient condition for knowledge (1992: 58). It is less than truth, since knowledge implies truth. But he claims that for an anti-realist – at least in those regions of discourse (and for a *global* anti-realist, in all regions) that are more response-dependent than others, such as ethics, comedy and perhaps mathematics, where truth does not exceed that to which we have *access* – superassertibility is also a sufficient condition for knowledge, hence that (K) becomes an equivalence:

(L) p *is superassertible iff* p *is knowable*

Now, as we have just seen, this line of thought is based on two assumptions: (a) that assertion implies warranted assertibility in a strong enough sense to imply its objectivity, although in a weak enough sense to imply that it is not knowledge (superassertibility), and (b) the conception of knowledge as true belief plus something that is conclusive justification (or as belief as a necessary but insufficient condition for knowledge). But at least the first assumption can be questioned.

On the usual view of assertion, sincere assertion expresses belief, and a belief is assertible only if it has a certain property. The most obvious candidate for this property is truth, and the norm or constitutive rule of assertion can be formulated:

(AT) *Assert* p *only if* p *is true*

(or its disquoted equivalent). But of course we often don't know what is true. So the rule is often broken, but this does not preclude us from following it (it does not say that *we assert* only truths, but that *we should assert* only truths). But if we are sensitive to the contingencies of the epistemic situations of subjects, we can take assertion to express not beliefs that we take to be true, but only beliefs as *warranted*. The rule would then be:

(AW) *Assert* p *only if you have warrant for* p

As we saw, the deflationist can accept either (AT) or (AW), provided that truth has a thin sense and is neither defined as transcending verification nor as immanent to it. A minimalist anti-realist like Wright can accept both too. Now there is a third possibility, which has been defended by several writers, in particular Peter Unger (1975) and Timothy Williamson (2000): assertion expresses something stronger than warrant, namely knowledge:

(AK) *Assert* p *only if you know that* p

Like (AT), this norm is often violated, but this does not preclude it from expressing the standard of assertion: to assert that *p* is to represent oneself as *knowing* that *p*. Knowledge is stronger than warrant, since it implies warrant, but is not implied by it. But knowledge implies truth, for to know that *p* implies that *p* is true. So (AK) implies (AT): the norm of truth is derivative from the norm of knowledge. But what grounds are there for (AK)?

There is, first, some linguistic evidence. When someone asserts something, and when we want to question that assertion, we say: "How do you *know*?" A second consideration is drawn from Moore's paradox (see §2.5). It is odd to say "*p* but I don't believe that *p*", but if an assertion expressed only warrant falling short of being knowledge, it should not be odd to say "*p* but I don't know that *p*" for one could have warrant to say this. But it is odd too: "France is hexagonal, but I don't know that it is" is certainly a bizarre assertion. But can't we assert things when we do not represent ourselves as knowing them? Can't we assert hypotheses, conjectures, guesses or mere hunches? There is no oddity in "*p*, but *p* is not warranted" when I take myself to express a guess, or in "*p*, but this just a conjecture." But here we should say that such statements do not really express assertions: we do not represent ourselves as *asserting* that *p*, but only as guessing that *p*. Similarly for fiction: if a text starts with "One upon a time . . .", we know at once that it is not in the assertive mode. As Frege says for such cases, they present simply mocked assertions.[24] Williamson (2000: 246) also invokes a further consideration from the case of lotteries. If I have bought a ticket out of 1,000 others in a lottery, I may have a very high probability (0.999) for believing that it will not win, but that does not entitle me to *assert* that it will not win. Even if my ticket, expectedly, does not win, you can criticize my assertion "It will not win" by saying: "But you did not *know* that it would not win", for on your evidence, I had only a very strong probability of not winning, but no knowledge of it. So it seems to go with the act of assertion that the speaker has a special authority, and not simply a claim to mere belief, over what is asserted.

That I *take* myself to know that *p* when I assert *p* does not imply that I *actually* know that *p*, just as that assertion *aims at* truth does not imply that what I assert *is* true. But it implies that assertion carries at least the potential to express knowledge, and not simply belief and warrant. Or rather, if assertion has the potential to express belief and warrant, it has also the potential to express knowledge. For we can take belief to be an attitude towards a proposition that we *cannot discriminate* from knowledge, or that we treat *as if* it were knowledge. This does not imply, of course, that belief *is* knowledge, or that knowing is mere believing, but only that, *for all one knows*, one can take one's beliefs as knowledge. We certainly say "I believe that *p*, but I don't know it", but this is perfectly compatible with the analysis that makes belief a claim to know, for we can take ourselves to believe, hence to pretend to know, without actually knowing. As Williamson says, belief is "botched knowledge" (2000: 46). Knowledge is the standard by which we judge ourselves to be believing, and when we express our beliefs linguistically, the standard of assertion. Now this presumption of knowledge, as we may call it, sets a standard for discourse that is much higher than mere warrant, but also much higher than superassertibility. For in aiming at knowledge we aim at truth (for knowledge implies truth), *in a verification-transcendent sense*: what we take to be knowledge might fail to be knowledge. As Williamson puts it: "The gap between what is true and what we are in a position to know is not a special feature restricted to some problematic areas of discourse; it is normal throughout discourse" (2000: 13). So our discourse, through permitting the expression of knowledge, imposes on us a *realist* standard, in Dummett's sense of the verification transcendence of our statements. This why I say that thesis 7 of MR implies a realist commitment. This commitment is implicit in our talk about truth, and in this sense it is a platitude.

But it is a platitude that has more weight than the truistic corre-spondence platitude, and more weight than the platitude that truth is not justification. Now, if this specific link between assertion, be-lief, knowledge and truth is a commitment of MR, doesn't that put the minimalist part of MR in jeopardy? In other words, haven't we allowed ourselves to "inflate" the minimalist norm of truth too much? Haven't we come back to *metaphysical* realism?

The answer is that by itself the intimate connection between assertion and knowledge is only presumptive of realism, and does not guarantee it.[25] It sets realism as the "default option", but it does not settle the status of realism or anti-realism in any region of discourse. It is open to us to discover that the realist presumption is not satisfied in some areas. Hence it does not settle the question of the truth-aptness of a given discourse. In this sense we are still with the minimal concept of truth, although I say, like Wright, that this concept is stronger than warranted assertibility. But I also say, unlike Wright, that it is stronger than superassertibility. What MR says is that minimal truth has the power of allowing our discourse to have verification-transcendent truth conditions. Whether it *has* it in all areas is a further question. In this sense, I want to deny that MR is committed to a particularly strong form of realism.

It is certainly possible to develop the account of assertion as based on knowledge into a full-blown realism. But then we will not simply need to criticize, as I did, the first assumption (a) above (assertion does not imply a claim to knowledge), but also the second (b) (knowledge is true belief plus something else). To do this would be to defend a realist theory of knowledge itself. This is what Williamson does. He takes knowledge to be a *mental state* (of the same category as attitudes such as seeing or remembering) different from belief, and claims that to know that *p*, one does not need to *believe* that *p* (against the traditional analysis of knowledge as justi-fied true *belief*). On this view, knowing is not being in a state of mind such as belief, plus a non-mental condition of believing truly. Rather, as suggested above, we should analyse believing in terms of (inappropriate) knowing. Williamson closely associates knowledge to reliability, and reliability to realist truth.[26] This expansion of MR into a full-blown realism is possible, but I do not think it is needed for MR. To assess this issue, we would have to go much deeper into the theory of knowledge.

A potential worry has not yet been addressed. One might ask: "If you accept that there is a realist presumption in all assertive discourses, but that this presumption will be either satisfied or not when one examines their truth-aptness, what will be the criterion for a realism about truth-*aptness*? How can this criterion fail to be the fact that such and such a discourse *corresponds to reality* or not? Hence aren't you committed to a robust realist theory of truth-aptness anyway?" The answer is a qualified yes. MR accepts a realist view of truth-aptness – which does not mean that one has to be a realist in all domains – but not a realism of the correspondentist kind. I shall come back to this at the end of Chapter 4.

The realist/anti-realist
4 controversies

Minimal realism, like Wright's minimalism, implies that the realist/ anti-realist issues will be distinct from domain to domain. In a sense, it is obvious. For the fact that one is, say, a realist in mathematics who takes numbers to be abstract entities belonging to a separate realm does not imply that one has to be a realist in ethics, for instance – by contrast with the purity of Cantor's paradise, the realm of human feelings might seem to us such a messy place that it does not allow us to take values as real entities – and an expressivist in ethics can well be a realist about scientific theories. One might think that the combination of realism in science and of anti-realism in the philosophy of mathematics is less obvious, for if mathematics is to be applied to the natural world, how can mathematical entities fail to be real?[1] But it is perfectly consistent with anti-realism in Dummett's sense, and with intuitionism, to accept a form of realism about the entities that science speaks about.[2] So one does not need to be a *global* realist or a global anti-realist in all areas. But it remains to be seen how this can happen in various domains and whether we can afford to have all the possible combinations. There are many such domains in philosophy today, not only those already mentioned, but every domain where we can ask whether truth-aptness may escape us, or where we can ask whether the very notion of *truth conditions* has sense. For instance we ask this question about *modality*: a modal realist is someone who not only takes for granted our talk of possibilities and necessities, but believes that there are deep modal facts. We can ask the question about *psychological* talk: are our beliefs, desires, and other intentional states *real*? About *conditionals*: do all sentences of the *if . . . then* form have truth conditions? About *fiction*: can there be truth in fiction? About *the past*: are statements about the past true? And so on. The stock in trade is large, and supplies a wide range of issues debated in contemporary philosophy.[3] It is difficult to think that the availability of a single framework to deal with the concept of truth will not have effects on each of them, but the very diversity of the issues makes it difficult to believe that a uniform treatment will be forthcoming. Here I shall confine myself only to three: theoretical truths in science, moral truths, and mathematical truths. At this stage, it is difficult for a book on truth not to expand itself into a book on realism in general, and on these particular issues, just as we have seen that it is difficult to prevent it from becoming a book on epistemology. I shall not attempt anything like this, but I shall have to say, although in a quite schematic form, something about the epistemology and the ontology of each of these three domains to have at least a partial confirmation of my proposal.

4.1 Theoretical truths in science

The traditional controversy about realism in science is often presented as a controversy about the nature of scientific theories as bearing upon a domain of *non-observable* entities such as mass, atoms or electrons. This controversy is between those who take these entities as real and the terms that refer to them as genuinely referential, and those who adopt *instrumentalism*, the thesis that scientific theories are just means of prediction that can be empirically adequate without describing a real world transcending our observational and predictive powers. Typically the controversy in that form consists, for the realist camp, in pointing out that certain basic features of our scientific practice, such as its explanatory power, its success and the indispensability of theoretical entities for this practice, cannot be accounted for without saying that our theories are *true*, or susceptible to be so. Typically, the instrumentalist camp retorts that only prediction matters, that theoretical entities can be eliminated or constructed out of only observable ones, and that the success of scientific practice can perfectly be explained without saying that theoretical statements are true. For instance, the realist will say that it would not be possible to get new and surprising predictions from our theories if they were only calculating devices, or that the explanatory success of science cannot be accounted for if it does not presuppose an underlying unified reality. The instrumentalist will retort that the practice of scientific prediction does not generate more true predictions than random predictions could so generate, that the novelty of some predictions does not imply the existence of hidden causes, that the unified character of science is a myth, and that simplicity is only a regulative maxim that does not imply that the structures of nature are themselves simple.

The realist/instrumentalist controversy about theoretical entities can seem to be centrally a dispute about truth, the realist deeming it indispensable, and the instrumentalist deeming it dispensable, or replaceable by such notions as assertibility, acceptability or verification. But it is not clear that the anti-realist paradigm in these debates offers a unified front against this rejection of the notion of truth. For an anti-realist about theoretical entities, who aims to reduce theoretical statements such as "There are electrons" to observable statements, might deny the truth of this statement, but not the truth of the corresponding translation of it in terms of observables.[4] The situation is exactly parallel with the opposition between the naïve realist about tables, chairs and material objects, and the phenomenalist who holds that these can be reduced to statements about sense data: for the reduction to go through, these statements about sense data have to be true. Hence although we can say that for a reductive anti-realist there are no truth conditions for theoretical statements, but only assertibility conditions in terms of observables, the statements that relate to the observables can very well be true or false. So it is not clear that the reductive phenomenalist or empiricist in the philosophy of science can completely get rid of the concept of truth.[5]

This applies also to views that are not, strictly speaking, reductionist, in that they do not reject the theory/observation contrast. For instance, Nancy Cartwright has argued in her appropriately titled book *How the Laws of Physics Lie*, that theoretical laws (such as the laws of thermodynamics) in physics are *false*, and that the phenomenological laws of the corresponding domain (merely describing the behaviour of bodies) are true. She calls her view[6] "*entity realism*" (see Cartwright 1983): we may believe in all sorts of entities posited by scientific theories (electrons, genes, etc.) while suspending belief in the truth of the theories in which they are embedded. It seems hard to say, however, that we could believe in electrons, but not in the theories about them, unless there is here an equivocation on the concept of "belief": it can be taken as an attitude to *truth-apt* statements (a form of judgement that things are thus and so) or as merely an *attitude* that does not carry the truth-aptitude of anything that can be the content of a belief (something like a mere *positing* of the relevant entities). If the former, Cartwright is a realist about phenomenological laws, but an anti-realist about theories. If the latter, she is closer to another kind of anti-realism, which denies that scientific laws and theories are truth-evaluable at all. Ramsey, Wittgenstein in his middle period and Ryle[7] proposed a view of this kind, when they said that laws of the universal form "All ϕ are ψ" are just "variable hypotheticals" of the form "If I meet a ϕ I shall treat it as a ψ" (Ramsey), "rules of inference" or "laws for the formation of propositions" (Wittgenstein), or "inference tickets" that do not themselves express genuine propositions (Ryle). As Ramsey (1990: 149) puts it, a law in this sense cannot be denied: "This cannot be negated but it can be disagreed with by one who does not adopt it." On such a view, which has in this sense an obvious analogy with the corresponding view in ethics, a law or a scientific theory taken as a set of laws does not *describe* any reality at all: such laws and theories are only *expressions* of our decisions to adopt them. We act merely *as if* they referred to an independent reality, and in this sense we *project* our decisions onto the world, but the laws are not in fact truth-apt. They have no factual content at all. We may call this the *expressivist* or *projectivist* conception of theories.[8]

Both reductivist empiricism and expressivism about theories have been widely associated with the anti-realist tradition of logical positivism, but it reappears elsewhere. Some contemporary philosophers of science, most notably Mary Hesse, have argued that the role of metaphors in science is not auxiliary or heuristic, but essential. Hesse claims that there is no principled distinction between literal scientific truth and metaphors, and that even theoretical statements can be said to be metaphorical. She nevertheless adds that metaphors have "cognitive significance" (Hesse 1966, 1984). As I have already suggested about a more sweeping thesis held by Derrida (who extends it to all discourses), there is a characteristic tension in this view, for to say that scientific theoretical statements are metaphorical implies that they are not literally true, or truth-apt, whereas to say that they have cognitive significance seems to mean that they contribute to knowledge, hence to the advancement of truth-seeking, and therefore that they can be truth-apt. So it is not clear that Hesse is an anti-realist expressivist about laws in the sense discussed above. A more squarely expressivist view has been espoused by Rorty.[9] According to Rorty, who follows Davidson in this,[10] metaphors do not have any special meaning apart from the literal meaning of the words that occur in them, hence they have no cognitive significance or content, although they can be useful for eliciting such contents. They have only certain effects on us, such as suggesting or prompting analogies and similarities. They do not convey any sort of truth, and hence are not truth-apt. This debate is quite interesting, because we should remember that Rorty is a deflationist about truth, and denies that scientific talk is true in the literal sense (§2.6). So he has no means to contrast literal scientific truths with metaphorical talk. He should, on the contrary, *agree* with Hesse that scientific talk is not literally true, but for a distinct reason: because scientific theories are only true in the sense that we *approve* of them!

Actually, deflationism also has the resources for "deconstructing" all these debates. Simply apply Ramsey's ladder. If a scientific theory says that there are electrons, then it is true that there are electrons. But if we cannot defend any substantive theory of truth, the debate between the instrumentalist and the realist, or between the expressivist and the realist, is undercut.[11] They can both agree that it is true that there are electrons, for there is, on the deflationist account, no difference between accepting the theory and accepting it as true.[12] The same applies to metaphors, although Rorty fails here to invoke his deflationism about truth. There is no harm in saying that it is true that the Catholic Church is a hippopotamus, for this just says that the Catholic Church is a hippopotamus. But of course this robs of any sense the attempt to make a distinction between metaphorical talk and literal talk in terms of their difference in truth-aptitude, just as it robs of any sense the realism/anti-realism controversy over theoretical entities in science.

Arthur Fine is, among philosophers of science, the one who has most systematically pursued this deflationist line of thought. He claims that the only sensible attitude that we can adopt about the truth and the reference of theoretical statements is the "natural ontological attitude" (NOA), which he defines in the following way:

> A distinctive feature of NOA that separates it from similar views currently in the air is NOA's stubborn refusal to amplify the concept or truth by providing a theory or an analysis (or even a metaphorical picture). Rather NOA recognises in "truth" a concept already in use and agrees to abide by the standard rules of usage   (Fine 1986: 133)

The concept of truth "already in use" is just the concept characterized by our familiar equivalence schema or by the disquotational schema. We need neither to appeal to a reality that would correspond to our theories, nor to reduce truth to acceptability or assertability in the anti-realist manner. There is, however, Fine claims, a "core position" on truth that is shared by all sides in this debate. Nobody denies that the world is constituted by unobservable natural kinds posited by well-confirmed scientific theories, and that these are true for the same reasons as those for which our ordinary statements about tables, chairs or houses are true. Perhaps, suggests Fine, the NOA and its core position was the one that Einstein meant to endorse when he said: "Physics describes reality, but we do not know what reality is. We only know it through its description by physics." This might seem deep, but it can be expressed in the deflationary platitudinous way: physics is true if and only if what it says corresponds to the reality that it describes. But the usual syndrome of the difficulties that we have met in the various versions of deflationism reproduces itself here. Suppose we take the disquotational version. Then truth will be a predicate of sentences such as "There are quarks", and relative to a language (the language of particle physics); but unless we accept that this language can be translated, how can we escape the threat of relativism? And if we accept that truth applies to propositions in use (as Fine seems to imply), then we shall presuppose that there is a common meaning of such sentences transcending various languages (including our ordinary talk), so that these languages talk about the same things. This, however, is a typical realist assumption. The questions about how we can translate a theory into another will be begged. NOA also threatens to undercut all epistemological questions about scientific theories. For scientists do not simply take their favourite theories as true because they take them to explain "reality" *in general*. They take them as true because they have *particular reasons* to accept them as true and as explanatory, within a given context. But NOA cannot accommodate this epistemological distinction. Fine denies that he is simply a deflationist about truth (1986: 184). But if he does not endorse this view, he will have either to adopt a form of anti-realism or instrumentalism of the kind that writers like Van Fraassen have advocated (Van Fraassen 1981), or to inflate NOA into a form of realism. It may be what his "core position" intends to capture. I suggest that it is what MR does. But MR does not prevent us from adopting a more robust form of realism in the scientific domain. I take it that one can, and should, adopt it, without suscribing to metaphysical realism. But this is not the place to argue for this.[13]

4.2 Truth in ethics

Things are in a sense simpler, but in another sense more complex, in the ethical domain. They are simpler, because the picture of a realm of moral facts or entities totally independent from us, and possibly undetectable, is today of very little appeal even to convinced moral realists, except perhaps those who intend to rely on theological premises. The usual realist metaphor of the discovery of entities the existence of which was unsuspected still has currency in mathematics or in physics, but it is hard to see what sense it could be given in the realm of human affairs. By definition, even if moral facts are conceived as detected by a faculty of intuition or through some special moral sense, they seem to be *essentially* detectable, and the idea that they could exist without ever being recognized is both unintelligible and useless. For if they had this undetectable mode of existence, how could they guide our conduct? Even if one holds the view that there are moral values, but that they are never instantiated in the world, one needs to have some idea of what they look like. In other words, in the realm of values, being and being known seem to go hand in hand. This is why the controversies in this field oppose various forms of realism that cannot be as strong as the ones that we could be prepared to accept in other areas to various forms of anti-realism. But flat-out anti-realism in ethics is also hard to accept, unless we side with pure relativism and scepticism, because the anti-realist owes us an account of why moral or ethical statements are not truth-apt. So in this sense the issues are more complex than in other areas.

The overall landscape, however, looks pretty much as it does elsewhere. If we characterize the debate between realism and anti-realism in ethics in terms of the notion of truth, the former is the view that ethical statements can be true or false, whereas the latter denies them this property. Let us call this the *semantic* dimension. But there is an internal complexity within each kind of view that can be characterized at three levels: *ontological* (what kind of entities or properties do ethical statements refer to?), *epistemological* (how can we know such entities?), and *practical or motivational* (how can they motivate us in our action?). The third level – how can ethical judgements lead us to actions? – is distinctive of the ethical domain, for there is no comparable requirement in the cognitive domain. To answer the ontological question, some moral realists hold that values, like the good, are real and intrinsic entities or properties that cannot be analysed in further terms, whereas some others hold that they can be so analysed, or shown to depend upon naturalistic properties (e.g. utility).[14] To answer the epistemological question, some moral realists hold that we know that ethical statements are true through some faculty of intuition or through some perception of moral facts. Others admit that this faculty is not something innate, but that it can in some sense be learnt through the exercise of various dispositions. To answer the motivational question, realists typically hold that some of our beliefs or judgements, those that contain moral or normative terms, have an intrinsic motivating power. The anti-realists counterattack on each dimension. They object that moral entities or properties would be "queer" or bizarre if it were admitted that they are "non-natural" properties;[15] that for the same reason they would be difficult to know through some intuition or perceptive faculty, and also it would be difficult to account for their motivational role. Here an argument derived from Hume's analysis of practical reasoning has been quite influential. According to the so-called "Humean theory of motivation", a mere belief has by itself no motivational role, for beliefs have only a representational role, and cannot move us to act, unlike desires. So how could moral *beliefs* differ in this respect?[16]

Moral realism is often called "cognitivism", because it takes moral facts to be genuine objects of knowledge. Moral anti-realism, because it denies this, is often called "non-cognitivism". But there are two distinct ways of understanding this latter phrase. On the one hand, we can say that the reason why moral facts are not known is that, although moral discourse has the power of express-ing truth or falsehoods, moral statements are simply *false*. If a fact is something that corresponds to a true proposition, there are, according to this view, no moral *facts*, hence no knowledge of what moral statements are about. This *"error theory"* of ethics has been defended by John Mackie (1977). What is distinctive in it is not only this striking claim, but also the denial of the semantic view that I have attributed above to the ethical anti-realist. Ethical statements are truth-apt, but they are false. If we remember, however, the pos-sibility of a view like Cartwright's about scientific realism, there is a similarity between it and Mackie's, although Mackie would deny that ethical statements could be true even at some "phenomeno-logical" level. The *esse* of moral properties cannot be their *percipi*, for there is nothing here to perceive.

The second way, on the other hand, of understanding "non-cognitivism" is in line with the semantic thesis that I have ascribed to ethical anti-realism: ethical statements are neither true nor false, they are not truth-apt. It is the expressivist paradigm that we have already encountered earlier. In a sense it is also an error theory, for it too holds that there are no moral properties. But the mistake, according to the expressivist, is due not to the fact that the world fails to contain the moral properties that our ethical statements pur-port to be about, but to the fact that they do not purport to be about anything. On the surface, however, ethical statements *seem* to be truth-apt, and to lend themselves to talk in terms of truth and falsity, but in their deep syntax, they do not. On the surface, statements like

(a) Bullfighting is wrong
(b) Playing cricket is right

can be assessed as true or false. They seem to have true negations, one can prefix "is true" or "is false" to them, disquote the resulting statements, and embed them within apparently truth-functional contexts such as "If bullfighting is wrong, then you should not attend the *corrida.*" In other words, they have the normal discipline of syntax that seems to fit the truth-predicate. But the expressivist tells us that these appearances are misleading: in fact, (a) and (b) do not describe anything, they do not even *report* the presence of subjective attitudes. They *express* or *voice* attitudes, feelings or emotions. In this respect, they are much more like performative statements, and we should read them in this way:

(a') Boo! (bullfighting)
(b') Hooray! (playing cricket)

where "boo!" and "hooray" are operators on the respective sentences (which fail to express *propositions*, since they are neither true nor false). This suggests that the underlying states are emotions, and this is often called the "boo–hooray" or "emotivist" theory of ethics, although it is not necessary that the states in question be emotions. The operators can be place-holders for all sorts of attitudes that are not representational, unlike beliefs: desires, feelings, or any sort of response that a subject might make. We could mark them, in Blackburn's (1998a) fashion, as positive or negative attitudes noted "↑" and "↓". But this strategy raises a well-known problem: (a) and (b), and their expressivist counterparts, are assertions. But when they are embedded, as is quite possible, as antecedents of conditional sentences, like "If *bullfighting is wrong*, then you should not attend the *corrida*", they occur *unasserted*: the italicized sentence here is not asserted. Nevertheless they have in such occurrences the same meaning as when they occur asserted. Moreover, they can occur in reasoning, like:

(a) Bullfighting is wrong
(b) If bullfighting is wrong, then you should not attend the *corrida*
(c) You should not attend the *corrida*

This is an instance of a straightforward *modus ponens* kind of argument (*if p then q, p, therefore q*). But even if we apply the expressivist analysis to (a) and (c), there is a problem with (b) since "Bullfighting is wrong" does not have the same meaning in (a) and in (b): so how can the argument go through and be valid, that is, be such that the *truth* of the premises is conserved in the conclusion?[17] The expressivist is bound to say that we do not really make moral arguments, but mere ejaculatory noises, or else reformulate the theory in order to account for the deep syntax of these arguments. The first strategy flies in the face of common sense, the second leads to very complex and cumbersome reformulations to the effect that argument-forms of the kind (a)–(c) are really expressive of some form of coherence within the attitudes of a subject (see Blackburn 1985, Gibbard 1990).

At this stage, we come back to familiar difficulties, which I have already raised above (§3.3) in the discussion of the difference between truth and truth-aptness. If expressivists say that ethical statements are not truth-apt (neither true nor false), and mean to contrast them with statements that make genuine assertions and that *are* truth-apt (sentences reporting beliefs that are genuinely representational), then they seem to be bound to say that, for the latter, truth is a real property, although it is not such a property for the former kind of statements. But if truth cannot be a real property of *any* kind of statement, they have no right to defend their view. Error theorists do not seem to face this problem, for they hold the semantic thesis that ethical statements are truth-apt, but that they are false. So they would have no problem with a reasoning such as (a)–(c) above, for they would just hold that the premises and conclusion are false. Nevertheless the falsity of ethical sentences is supposed to be evaluated in terms of some standard of correspondence with fact. Real objective values are just not there to fulfil the apparently referential role that ethical sentences have. In other words, ethical sentences are not only false, but robustly so. But this is just what deflationism denies. Some expressivists, however, like Ayer, hold both an emotivist view of ethics *and* a redundancy theory of truth. But as we have seen from Boghossian's argument (§3.3), there is an obvious tension between these positions. So moral anti-realists should not welcome the deflationist or minimalist theory of truth. True deflationists should not be anti-realists. They should say: "Of course, our ethical statements are true or false. So what?" and adopt a relaxed attitude. But if there is no way of distinguishing description of matters of fact from expression of attitudes, any sort of meta-ethical view, be it realist or anti-realist, is absurd.

The gist of these objections has already been given in our discussion of truth and truth-aptness in §3.3 above. It can be summarized by saying that it must be one thing to be a deflationist or minimalist about *truth*, and another thing to be a minimalist about *truth-aptness*. If this is so, an anti-realist of the expressivist kind can perfectly accept the former, and reject the latter. Simon Blackburn, one of the main contemporary expressivists, does just that (see Blackburn 1998a; cf. M. Smith 1994a). He agrees that "true", in many areas, and in ethics in particular, signals our commitments to certain propositions, and our endorsement of those of others, and that a thin truth-predicate syntactically disciplined is perfectly in order for this, but he claims that spelling out the *nature* of these commitments is a different story. Blackburn here is perfectly faithful to Ramsey, who, remember (§2.4), said that although there is no separate problem of truth, there is a separate problem for *belief*. There is indeed a minimalist story to tell about belief as well as about truth: that assertions express beliefs, that denials express rejection or disbelief, that to believe that *p* is to believe that *p* is true, and so on. But it is not a minimal matter whether or not a state is a state of belief (see also Jackson *et al.* 1994: 296). For instance, it is not trivial that beliefs are functional states resulting from our informational relations with the world and cause actions, whether they are conscious or tacit, dispositional or not. And, to take up the issue raised by the "Humean" theory of motivation, it is not a trivial fact, but a disputed one, that beliefs are only representational states, which cannot, unlike desires, move us to act.

The task set by the expressivist is to show how our patterns of positive or negative attitudes are constituted, and then to try to relate this pattern to our commitments, by understanding how the underlying structure of our feelings can be connected with the surface features of our discourse about moral properties. This connection has been called by Blackburn, following Hume, a kind of *projection* of mind onto the world: we feel, love, hate, accept, reject certain things, and this pattern is then projected so as to yield claims about moral truths, ethical propositions, moral reasonings, and so on. The phenomena are saved, but the deep structure is quite distinct. This is why Blackburn calls his view a *quasi-realism*: in ethics in particular, things are *as if* there were real values, although there aren't. This does not prevent us from keeping our discourse about them just as it is. Quasi-realism is obviously more satisfactory than an error theory, because it does not have to say that "Bullfighting is wrong" is an instance of an error or of a particular superstition. It is also much more satisfactory than pure deflationism, for quasi-realists do not simply content themselves with the claim that moral statements are true – assertible – in the same sense as statements about matters of fact. Of course, all this will imply that we can draw the line between those attitudes which, perhaps like beliefs or judgements, are truth-apt in a robust sense (say, because they represent features of reality) and those which, like feelings or emotions, are not. But will drawing this line not imply that we should have criteria of robustness, for instance, correspondence with reality, to sort out the former from the latter? Similarly for metaphor: even if we might accept that metaphorical talk satisfies superficially minimalist standards for truth (e.g. Romeo can say: "It's true that Juliet is the sun", or "If Juliet is the sun then she dazzles me"), at one point or another we shall need to provide a criterion for distinguishing literal talk from metaphorical talk. This is not, however, an impossible task. In the case of metaphor, one can, like Davidson, say that literal meaning is given by the usual conventions of language, and that metaphorical sentences are literally *false*, an observation that leads us to look elsewhere for their meaning than in this literal sense: in the intentions that speakers want to express. But doesn't this talk of literal truth and falsehood betray a realist sense of the predicate "true", contrary to what minimalism says? The answer is yes but, on the view defended here, this is what we should expect. Once again, an expressivist need not be a minimalist about truth-*aptness*. At this level, one can be, like Blackburn, an anti-realist (or a sophisticated "quasi-realist"). But, alternatively, one could also be a realist or a cognitivist. Such a view, it seems to me, is compatible with the minimal realist conception that I have advocated: minimal realism at the level of truth ascriptions and non-minimal realism – realism *tout court* – at the level of truth-aptness.

Minimalists of the kind defended by Wright will, however, find that all this just begs the question. For, they will say, the problem of the robustness of the truth-predicate is transferred at the level of truth-aptness. At this second level, Wright also defends a minimal anti-realism. He actually claims that within moral discourse the truth-predicate is throughout the predicate of superassertibility (1992: 58, 60, 1996b).[18] Morality is a matter of trying to reach a justification of our moral beliefs that falls short of being a perfect or ideal justification, but that attempts to reach some sort of equilibrium where these beliefs will not be overthrown easily (are superassertible). There is no hope, on this view, of making moral truth something more than a convergence on our responses, and no hope of considering moral truth as the description of an externally robust reality. Wright's conception of ethical truth, although it is anti-realist, will accommodate some cognitivist intuitions. Full-blown cognitivists on one side, and quasi-realist expressivists on the other, will, of course, disagree. But I take it that this further disagreement can be understood as well from a minimal anti-realist conception, such as Wright's, as from a minimal realist one, such as that proposed here. I have claimed above that there is an intimate connection between truth and the norm of knowledge. This should lead us to a view that is more cognitivist than expressivist in kind. One way or another, it would have to confront the problem of motivation raised by the Humeans, and to explain how a knowledge of moral truths can lead us to act upon them. This is not the place to develop such an account, and I must content myself with indicating a possible line to take.[19]

4.3 Mathematical truth

Let us finally turn to the case of mathematical truths. Here again we shall deal mostly with taxonomies. It will be useful, in order to map out the terrain, to distinguish a variety of questions.[20] First we have the question:

(1) *Should mathematical statements be appraised as true or false?*

The answer "no" does not seem to be available, and in this respect there does not seem to be any equivalent of expressivism in ethics for mathematics: no one holds the absurd view that in doing mathematics we just voice our feelings.[21] But on reflection this is too quick. The school known as *formalism* holds that pure mathematical statements do not have truth-evaluable contents. They are just marks or signs that we manipulate according to certain rules.

But formalism is not the only option. Wittgenstein has held that in mathematics we do not really make judgements, but formulate rules for the use of these concepts.[22] A theorem, in this sense, does not state a truth, but gives us some rule or instruction for the use of a concept in inferences. In this sense a theorem is like an imperative: "Do it *that* way!" This seems to be as close to an expressivist view in ethics as one can think of.[23] On the other side, there are whole series of realist options as well as anti-realist options, which answer the question:

(2) *Are mathematical statements true in a substantial sense?*

There are at least three ways of answering "yes" and siding with the realist camp. The traditional *Platonist* answer says that certain kinds of abstract objects, which do belong to space and time, are the truth-makers of mathematical truths. But we can conceive of other abstract objects, and a prominent second kind of answer has been that *structures* can be appropriate candidates for abstract objects, instead of numbers or classes, for instance. A third answer is this. At least certain schools of *intuitionism* hold that mathematical truths are made true by mental or psychological states. But it is not clear that such a view can count, like the other ones, as "realist", if the mental objects are not mind independent. Among those who answer "no" to (2), there are, again, two camps. On the one hand, there are a variety of *constructivist* views, which say that mathematical statements are not true, but warrantedly assertible. On the view that all mathematical problems should be solved with set square and compass, constructivism comes close to the Wittgensteinian thesis that mathematical truths are instances of rule-following, and, given that a rule applies only to a finite domain, this view is often called *strict finitism*. The specific kind of assertibility in mathematics is here proof or demonstration. Now if we conceive of proofs as mental constructions, then the intuitionists are more on this side. On the other hand, there are a variety of reductionist views, according to which the truth of mathematical statements is a matter of their purported objects being reduced to other kinds of entities. This is the *nominalist* option: it says that mathematical statements are not made true by abstract objects, but by individual entities. There is a version of nominalism, recently defended by

Hartry Field (1981, 1993), which is parallel to Mackie's error theory in ethics, and also, in a sense, to Cartwright's view of theories in empirical science: it says that *pure* mathematical statements are all false, although their nominalistic equivalents and *applied* mathematics (mathematics applied to physics, or to empirical science in general) are true (compare with what Cartwright says of phenomenological laws).

The logical space of possibilities is not, however, limited to these. It is clear that the answers to (2) are constrained by the answers to:

(3) *How can mathematical propositions be known to be true?*

Platonists typically appeal to a special kind of intuition, anti-realists to our knowledge of proofs, nominalists to our knowledge of how our mathematical statements are applied to physical reality, and so on. But it is not as if question (3) were separate from the others. There is, for each account, a special problem of how to reconcile a certain conception of what makes mathematical statements true (their ontology) with a conception of how they can be known (their epistemology). This involves answering a certain kind of challenge, which has been formulated by Paul Benacerraf: (a) if mathematical entities are of the sort that Platonists believe in, that is, abstract objects independent of the mind, then how can we know them? (b) but on any plausible view of knowledge, it must imply some appropriate causal contact with the objects, (c) hence how can Platonists reconcile their ontology of abstract objects with this causal requirement in epistemology (Benacerraf 1973)? Benacerraf's challenge is set initially for the Platonist, but *any* view in the philosophy of mathematics must in some sense give us both a plausible ontology and a plausible corresponding epistemology. Anti-realists are on safer ground with the latter, since for them mathematical truths are essentially *known*. But then how can they account for those parts of mathematics that deal with the infinite, and for the phenomenon of mathematical discovery, which seems fitter to the well-known metaphor of a yet unknown land that we discover than to the metaphor of invention? Similarly, although nominalists seem to have the epistemology right, their economical ontology seems to account badly for the rich structures of mathematics. Benacerraf's challenge can be considered as giving the impetus for various views. Benacerraf himself took it as a motive for adopting a certain structuralist view of numbers as structures or patterns, rather than as objects (Benacerraf 1973, Resnik 1997). Other forms of realism accept the ontology of abstract objects, such as numbers and classes, but claim that they do not have to be postulated as the objects of a mysterious intuition, because they are indispensable within the rest of our scientific theories, in particular in physics. This is Quine and Putnam's "indispensability thesis" about the existence of mathematical entities (Quine 1970, Putnam 1971). But there are other ways of accommodating a Platonist ontology within a naturalistic account of knowledge. Some ontological realists, like Penelope Maddy, claim that mathematical knowledge is a form of causal knowledge, by which sets and numbers are known through ordinary perception (and not through some mysterious intuition) (Maddy 1990).

Expectedly, there is an easy way of reconciling all sides in these ontological and epistemological disputes: deflationism about mathematical statements. Its crudest formulation will, once again, take the form of the disquotational schema. To say, that, for instance "$7 + 5 = 12$" is true is just to say:

$$\text{"}7 + 5 = 12\text{" is true iff } 7 + 5 = 12$$

No need to talk of abstract objects. Sentences are enough. Now if we remember the strictures on a disquotational theory, this will have to be relativized to a given set of mathematical sentences, or to a mathematical theory. And if we want to take into account our knowledge of these truths, we could just say that the simple arithmetical truth "$7 + 5 = 12$" is relative to our current mathematical knowledge. An adaptation of Fine's NOA could be done for mathematics: mathematical statements are true when they are considered as knowledge by the working community of mathematicians. But here difficulties creep in. For to have the disquotational sentence above in proper form, one needs to be sure that the notion of truth will not reappear on the right-hand side. But this means that there is a way of spelling out the acceptance of "$7 + 5 = 12$" without mentioning truth. One can do this by using only such notions as consistency and proof, where a set of sentences are consistent if and only if one does not meet one sentence and its negation, and where a set of sentences are proved from others when they can be derived by the means of rules of inference. But can it be done? Hilbert's programme in the foundations of mathematics tried to do it. But Gödel's second incompleteness theorem tells us that there are in mathematics certain sentences that are true, but that cannot be proven to be true. If this is so, how could the proper deflationist option be taken? Note that this problem is not specific to a deflationist: it arises also for an anti-realist of a constructivist kind, who takes truth to be proof or assertibility.[24] There is worse. I have mentioned Field's error theory, according to which all statements of pure mathematics are false. He combines it with a deflationist theory of truth, both for natural language in general and for mathematics (Field 1993: Ch. 4).[25] But how can Field defend this view if he also holds that pure mathematics is false? For he will have to have, like the expressivist or the error theorist in ethics, a certain view about truth-*aptness*, a view about what distinguishes what he calls "factually defective discourse" from non-factually defective discourse.

Wright's own way with these issues is a combination of his disciplined syntacticism for truth and a minimalist conception of truth-aptness. The first component of his view is the claim that what makes mathematical discourse a candidate for truth-aptness is a set of syntactic criteria: in the case of numbers, the criterion is that number terms are singular terms and function as such, and that they can be subjects of certain predications that figure in identity statements. Further from that, there is no question of whether such number terms do refer to genuine entities. Numbers are objects only in so far as they can be *named*. This can be understood as a form of Platonism, but only of a "syntactic" kind.[26] The second component in Wright's view is a conception of truth as proof. Mathematical statements are true in so far as they can be proved as such. But here truth is not mere assertibility. It is superassertibility, and in this respect mathematics is on a par with ethics, which is also, for Wright, basically a discourse where the minimal concept of truth is superassertibility. Wright's hope, here as elsewhere, is to reconcile the objectivity of mathematical statements with an epistemic conception of truth as proof. This view is certainly on the anti-realist side. If truth outruns proof, as the Platonist traditionally claims, the anti-realist will not be convinced. Wright's minimal anti-realism certainly provides a way of accommodating our basic intuitions about truth within an anti-realist framework that is more satisfactory than an error theory or a deflationist conception of mathematical truth, but it does not settle the basic disagreement between Platonists – or realists in general– and their constructivist opponent.

4.4 Realism vindicated

Let us try to take stock. I have briefly reviewed only three, although important, areas where questions about truth and realism classically arise. In all of them we have the same patterns of commitments: a minimal truth-concept conforming to the requirements of truth-aptitude, syntactic discipline and satisfaction of the truth-platitudes. This justifies a minimalist view about truth, as resting upon a core concept applicable to each domain of discourse. But in each case, the issues about truth-*aptness*, although they manifest strong similarities, do not arise in the same way as in the other cases. This suggests that truth is a functional property, variably realized in each case. In this respect, the view proposed here, MR, has much in common with Wright's minimalist programme. But it is not committed to the idea that, for most discourses, a weaker predicate than realist truth, superassertibility, is operative. On the contrary, I have claimed that given that the norm of truth is a norm of knowledge, the truth-predicate is the verification-transcendent realist concept of truth. This gives us something like the taxonomy of the various minimalist positions shown in Figure 4, distinguishing two levels of minimalist commitments, respectively at the level of truth and at the level of truth-aptness. Now, the questions left open at the end of §3.5 still arise: doesn't that mean that MR is simply the view that our concept of truth is the realist concept? If so, how can the minimalist project be maintained? Another way of putting these questions is to remark that minimal realism and anti-realism occur in Figure 4 at the two levels, the level of truth and the level of truth-aptness, but that MR does not occur at the second level (answer 2.2 "no" to our question). Isn't there a tension here?

MR says, unlike Wright's minimal anti-realism, that you can afford to be a minimalist about truth, but that you cannot afford to

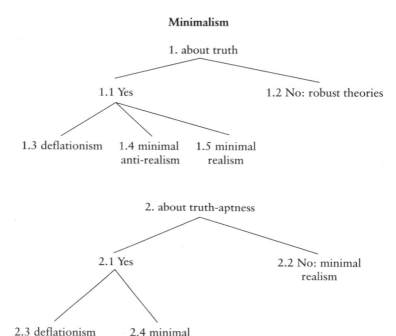

Figure 4

be a minimalist about truth-aptness. This means that, when it comes to the actual meaning of truth claims in a given domain, we need a robust conception of the truth *conditions* of sentences in this discourse. As we have seen, for instance, for ethics, either you need to say that ethical statements have truth conditions, and you are a cognitivist, or you need to say that they are not, in which case you are an expressivist. But a conception of truth *conditions* can hardly be alien to a conception of *truth*, for how could one fail to have a conception of these conditions, without having a conception of *what* they are the conditions *of*? Remember David Wiggins's question raised at the end of §3.1 above: if we have a T-predicate f for a proposition, how can we fix the meaning of f without presupposing that it denotes *truth* itself, namely that it is a *truth*-predicate? So, either you have to be a minimalist *all the way down*, for both truth and truth-aptness, or you have to be a substantive theorist of truth all the way down too. This seems to put in jeopardy a conception like MR, which combines a minimalist at the first level with a non-minimalism at the second level.

But I don't think that MR is so threatened. The reason why you need to have a robust conception of truth conditions is, as we have seen in §3.3 above, that minimalism about truth-aptness robs all sorts of debates of any sense. We have seen that expressivism, if we cannot distinguish a robust from a thin notion of truth conditions, is deprived of any bite. Perhaps it is so deprived, but if so there is not scope for distinguishing a realist from an anti-realist conception within a given domain. All sorts of expressivism in ethics, but also in mathematics (e.g. Wittgenstein's position) and in science (e.g. Cartwright's position), will turn out to traffic with minimally truth-apt contents. Contrary to what minimalism about truth-aptness tells us, the realist/anti-realist options will not be open. Now a minimalist *à la* Wright will disagree with this, maintaining that error theorists or expressivists can still disagree that a discourse is genuinely assertoric if they are minimalist about truth-aptness. But I myself do not see why. For if they also accept disciplined syntacticism, they will have to agree that ethical discourse provides us with *correct* or *incorrect* assertions. Wright's framework licenses further criteria for deciding the realist/anti-realist issues (cognitive command and width of cosmological role). But he does not take cognitive command to license a realist view. It only "marks one step on the road towards vindication of a broadly realist conception of a discourse". So although it may be a necessary condition for realism, it not sufficient. But then what will be the further criteria if not criteria for robust truth-aptness?[27]

If we want, on the contrary, to leave the realist/anti-realist issues open, we have to make room for a robust conception of truth-aptness. Issues about truth-value gaps would be otherwise empty. For instance, we may want to know whether vague sentences, such as "John is bald", are really truth-apt or not. Issues in the theory of reference, such as for instance the problem of non-denoting terms and fictional discourse, are not solved just by saying that the corresponding sentences are truth-apt in the minimalist sense. Issues about the nature of belief too cannot be side-stepped so easily. We shall have to pro-vide criteria for distinguishing a state that is a belief, and that has representational powers, from states that do not. Otherwise the question that divides realists and "Humeans" in the theory of motivation about whether a belief can *by itself* have motivating powers will be robbed of its significance. Similarly, we shall have to provide criteria for an appropriate theory of *meaning*. Otherwise the issue whether meaning is a matter of truth conditions or of assertibility conditions, which divides realists from anti-realists in this field, will be empty. As I remarked about Horwich's views above (§2.4), he is consistent in saying that his deflationism about truth also needs a deflationary conception of *meaning*, and it is a genuine issue whether meaning is a matter of truth conditions, assertibility conditions or "use conditions". But if this is so, there is, here again, substantial room for debate. Not only should there be room for disagreement on these issues, but there are good reasons, as we have seen, to say that in order to assess realist and anti-realist debates, we need to say more than what the minimalist says about meaning, belief and knowledge, if knowledge is the standard of assertion. So we have to adopt a robust conception of truth-aptness, that is, to say that having genuine truth conditions makes a difference. Within the philosophy of meaning, reference and belief, there are a number of ways of spelling this out. For instance, informational or teleological semantics can provide criteria for semantic states to represent reality, causal or non-causal theories of reference can be provided, functionalist theories or conceptual role theories of belief and concepts can do that for beliefs, or a Davidsonian theory of interpretation, and so on. In other words, in all these domains, and in others – in ethics, in mathematics, in science, and so on – there must be some explanation of why a satisfactory account of meaning, belief, interpretation, ethical judgement, and so on can settle the application of the truth-predicate in each domain. And it is difficult to ask for an *explanation* if the criteria for truth-aptness are not robust or substantive.[28]

But now for the other horn of the dilemma: doesn't that mean that our concept of truth has to be robust or substantive *all the way up*, hence that we have to give up minimalism about truth? If truth-aptness is a property of truth, and if truth-aptness is robust, must not we conclude that truth is itself robust and revert to a substantive conception? No, for two reasons. The first is that an enquiry about truth-aptness in a given domain does not prevent us from sorting out the basic properties of the truth-predicate across each domain, and of its associated norms and platitudes, and we still say that it has the very "thin" features that the minimalist emphasizes. We can agree that "true" has no explanatory sense in itself, but signals that a given domain is in need of explanation. We say "It's true that lying is wrong." But that does not by itself vindicate moral realism. What vindicates it, or not, is a theory about rightness and wrongness. The second reason is that we do not need to accept that our criteria of truth-aptness answer the criteria of a substantive theory of truth in the classical sense examined in Chapter 1. In particular a realist concept of truth, or an anti-realist one, need not imply that truth-aptness is a matter of *correspondence* to reality or to facts in any substantial sense. The result of our discussion in Chapter 1 has been that there is no way to specify a notion of fact or correspondence apart from the notion of a true proposition. But that does not mean that truth-aptness is not a genuine property registering how things are in the world. For it is associated with specific norms: that propositions that are true are those that are susceptible to be known, although we might fail to know them (hence that it transcends our verifications). If the objections presented to deflationism and minimalism about truth are correct, in order to understand the concept of truth we need to rely on a rich pattern of usage that makes a given sentence a proposition, hence something that is truth-apt. But we may not be able, in all cases, to specify this pattern in terms that explain a certain sort of correspondence between our propositions and reality. For instance, to say that a man is bald can fail to have precise truth conditions, and this is why such utterances lend themselves to paradoxes of the sorites kind. We do not know which precise distribution of hairs make a sentence like "You are bald" true. But for all that the sentence can correspond to reality, or fail to do so, although we do not know exactly how. It may be that many of our ascriptions of truth are of this kind. But there is a question as to whether we do understand such sentences.[29] And if we can have a conception of what it is to believe something, as opposed to having an affective attitude towards it, then there is a question as to whether our moral judgements are reports of the former or expressions of the latter. I suggest that "corresponds to reality" can still have a sense without our needing to specify precise correspondence conditions.[30]

Where does this approach to the realist/anti-realist issues leave us? Dummett's influential approach to these issues consisted in

questioning our conceptions of truth and meaning in each appropriate area, by transforming realism and anti-realism into distinctive *semantic* theses. Minimalism in general takes a different line. It
accepts the idea that our *concept* of truth need not be readily realist
or anti-realist, but that it conforms, in most discourses, to the
requirements of the syntax of the truth-predicate and to the norms
of the respective discourses. But miminal anti-realism and minimal
realism, unlike deflationism, allow that the realist/anti-realist
debates are not meaningless. Minimal realism says that they occur
at the level of the truth-aptness of a discourse and takes the distinction between truth conditional and non-truth conditional discourse
seriously. At the level where the functional property of truth is
supposed to be realized, there is an issue as to whether this property
is realized or not. In this sense, there is a realist criterion of truth-
aptness, and one can have different conceptions of the properties
that are in place in science, in ethics, in mathematics, or elsewhere.
Since truth-aptness is aptness for *truth*, we have a realist conception
of it. Hence minimal realism, after all, is more realist than it is minimal. This is why it is located at 2.2 in Figure 4. It follows that the
debate between a realist and an anti-realist conception of truth is a
genuine, meaningful issue. In this sense, after all, Dummett's
approach is vindicated, although MR does not claim that the realist/
anti-realist issues rest only on semantic issues. In the end, it turns
out to be a matter of what kind of properties we countenance.

We could be tempted to conclude that the realist/anti-realist
debate, as it was traditionally formulated as an ontological debate
about what kinds of things and properties there are, is also vindicated. But this is not completely the case. For an enquiry about
truth cannot be led only at the level of what kinds of things there
are in the world, as if truth were one of them. (This would perhaps
be the case if truth could be explained through the relation of truth-
making, in Armstrong's sense for instance (§1.2)). But although
minimal realism is a realism in the sense that there are verification-
transcendent truths, truth is not a property that is "out there" in the
world, like tables, chairs or lakes. It is a property *of* propositions, of
things that are thought, believed or known. In this sense truth is an
epistemic *concept*, although truth is not an epistemic *property*. The
questions that belong to the category of the realist/anti-realist
disputes are also, in this sense, questions about the nature of the

concepts that are in place in each area: for example, physical, mathematical, ethical, fictional, modal, psychological, temporal and spatial concepts. The realist/anti-realist controversies are, on the one hand, about how each of these concepts are individuated, that is, how we come to know them, and on the other, about the truth of the statements involving these concepts. As in Benacerraf's challenge about the compatibility of a possible epistemology of mathematical truths and a possible ontology of mathematical objects, what we have to do in each case is to reconcile our epistemology of the concepts in each domain with the account of the truth of propositions involving them. At the end of the day, therefore, a theory of truth should not be married only with an ontology of knowledge, but with a theory of knowledge. It is there that truth becomes "substantive". I have not shown how this can be done, but just indicated how we could think of the connections between these questions within the framework of minimal realism.[31]

5 The norm of truth

We have been dealing mostly with what truth is, or is not, but we have not yet said very much about the *point* of the concept of truth, what truth is *for*, and what role it plays in our lives. Nobody, not even a deflationist, disagrees that it plays a role, and that the concept of truth is useful. If we look at the function of truth in a naturalist setting, there is no doubt that it has been important for our evolutionary histories that we were creatures able to have true rather than false beliefs, able not only to represent our environment correctly, but also to represent the beliefs of others, in order to predict their actions. As linguistic creatures, it is also quite important for us not only to have various ways of expressing our beliefs, but also to group them together, to refer to them, and to be able to distinguish truth-tellers from liars. But does that license us to say that truth is the goal of our inquiries, that the search for truth is an ultimate theoretical aim, or even an ultimate practical objective, the very foundation of wisdom? Many philosophers, in this sense, who are prepared to follow Aristotle when he says, at the very beginning of the *Metaphysics*, that "all men by nature desire to know" (*Metaphysics*: A, 980a21), are more reluctant to follow him when he says, at the end of the *Nicomachean Ethics*, that "perfect happiness is a certain theoretical activity" (*Ethics*: X, 1178b 7). It is one thing to say that we are trying to have true beliefs, and quite another to say that there is something, truth, to which our beliefs "aim at". It looks like the sort of fallacy denounced in all logic manuals, of passing from "For everyone there is something that he or she must search for" to "There is something for which everyone must search".[1] Not only the unity of the something searched for is problematic, but also the nature of the "must". I am concerned in this chapter to try to answer such doubts.

5.1 Truth and normativity

I have said that truth is a norm (§§3.1, 3.5). But this is a very confusing notion. A norm is something that allows us to issue imperatives of the form "You should φ" or "You ought not to ψ". Haven't I introduced a problematic and unnecessary "should", "ought", or "must"? Not only is this problematic because one does not see why there would be an obligation to search for truth, rather than something else, say happiness, success, creativity, or more mundanely money, pleasure, glory, or whatever, but also because it is not even clear that there is any imperative, or rule, to follow anything. Our thoughts, beliefs and statements are true or false. That is a property (light or weighty, it does not matter) that they have. Granted, it is better to have more true than false beliefs, overall, and, as a species that has survived, we have had more true than false ones, for otherwise we would not be here to think about it. But these are *facts*, on the "*is*" side of the *is/ought* distinction. What have duty, obligation, or normativity, which are on the "*ought*" side, to do with it? Haven't we passed "imperceptibly", as Hume says famously, from *is* to *ought*? Logicians talk of "true" or "false" as "truth-values". But that does not mean that truth is a value in anything more than the semantic sense. And even if we accept that truth is in some sense a norm, in what sense is it a norm? There are all sorts of norms: norms for playing games, for cooking, for marriage and other social activities. Is truth one of them? But then what kind of prominence could it have? You like to play cricket, I like to play the truth-game. So what? Is there something wrong with you but right with me? Norms are often practical, norms for action. But is truth a *practical* goal? That sounds absurd, if truth is a property of what we believe. For are our beliefs kinds of actions? Or should we say that truth is an epistemic or theoretical norm, just a norm for believing? But then, again, what kinds of obligations does it lead to? And what is the status of these obligations with respect to other obligations? If I ought to believe what is true, and if I ought also, say, to save a life, should I obey the first obligation at the expense of the other? These are all the obvious questions that the claim that truth is a norm raises.

It is important, therefore, when we say that truth is a norm, to see whether there is an *ought* present, implicitly or explicitly, and of what kind. We should also say whether the normativity that is supposed to be present in truth is an *essential* feature, which *exhausts* the meaning of this concept, or whether it is only an accidental or a secondary property of this concept. I said above that truth is a *constitutive* and *essential* norm of assertion. But why should we suppose that it is essential? If we compare assertion, like Dummett, to a game, and if we say that truth is the aim of this game, why could assertion not be "played" with other games? After all, liars and sophists play it with other aims than truth telling. And we could play it for all sorts of other aims: gossip, literature, poetry, and so on. Why suppose that truth is *central* to assertion? The deflationist has room for manoeuvre here. We utter a lot of sentences, with different aims, and each plays a different role (this is part of the Wittgensteinian image of language as a collection of different games). There is also some vagueness and "family resemblance" between games. Which one are we playing? Moreover, even if we suppose that some games are games of truth telling, a disquotationalist can argue that there is an infinite disjunction (in the form of DS* of §2.2) of sentences, all of which can be quoted by appending "is true" to them, this predicate registering what we may call, if we want to, a distinct "norm" in each case, without there being any "norm of truth" common to all cases. In the case of assertion, the norm has the form (AT) (§3.5): *Assert p only if p is true.* But certainly assertions are speech acts, and even if we agree that the truth rule (AT) is the central or essential rule of assertion, languages are contingent objects, and sometimes the act of assertion can be performed without using language, by gestures, signs or other conventions, although it is unclear that these are not parasitic upon the possibility of issuing linguistic assertions.

To these objections to the centrality of the norm of truth one can give two answers. The first is that the analogy between sentences and games only works if we consider isolated sentences. We combine sentences in order to make more complex ones, whose truth conditions are determined by the truth conditions of the simpler ones. Comparatively, there is no game of which both cricket and tennis are constituents. The compositionality of sentences forbids the disquotationalist move (see above §2.2).[2] The second answer is that, even if assertions could be disconnected in their aims, the normal role of assertion, including its role in lying, is to express the contents of one's *beliefs*. So the primary norm is not a norm linking truth and assertion, but a norm linking truth and *belief*. It seems extremely implausible to suggest that there might be as many different ways of believing and as many norms for belief as there are contents of beliefs. We would have to say that you do not believe in the same way when you believe that grass is green and when you believe that snow is white. The main reason why there has to be a central norm of truth is that belief *in general* aims at truth. But how are we to spell out the norm for beliefs? One way to cash the common idea that belief aims at truth is the following

(1) *If it is true that* p, *then one ought to believe that* p

For instance,

> If it is true that snow is white, then one ought to believe that snow is white

and, generalizing

(2) *For all* p, *if it is true that* p, *then one ought to believe that* p

But if this is the norm of belief, it is absurd. I can certainly incur no obligation to believe anything whatsoever that is true. For instance, there are a lot of truths contained in the phone book for the city of Paris, but these are not truths that I am required to believe, unless I want to play some game for testing my memory. What is important is that I believe truths when they are *relevant*, or interesting for a given task. And anyway, it is dubious that it is *required*, unless it is specified that the body of relevant beliefs is essential for a certain task (if I am a detective looking for suspects in a street, believing all the truths about the addresses might be required). So (2) can certainly not be a categorical "ought", but at best a contextual or hypothetical one, relative to some further aim.

A more adequate formulation of the norm of belief comes from the observation that the phrase "belief aims at truth" indicates that it is the function of belief to reach true, rather than false, contents. It is part of the "direction of fit" of beliefs: when a person has a false belief, and realises it, then, all things being equal, it is rational for that person to try to revise the belief and get a true one. However, when someone discovers that his or her desire can't be satisfied, there is not a similar rational requirement of changing the desire. So the idea is that we should believe only the things that we deem true. Then the norm, in *ought* form, for belief, is rather this:

(BT)   For *any* p, *one ought to believe that* p *only if* p *(is true)*.[3]

This time it makes perfectly good sense. (BT) does not imply, unlike (2), that we should believe any truth whatsoever. This imperative, in a sense, is quite obvious. It follows from the fact that claims to believe are claims to true beliefs, and from the conceptual constraint (highlighted by Moore's paradox) that to believe that *p* is to believe that *p* is *true*. Of course, the norm (BT) is often violated, but this is the case with every norm. It doesn't prevent the existence of cases of irrational belief formation, such as wishful thinking or self-deception, where someone can believe that *p* by some devious route, while believing, or knowing, that *p* is false. I have, however, argued above (§3.5), that claims to believe, and assertion, only make sense relative to a standard of *knowledge*. So I think that (BT) should more appropriately be formulated in the following form:

(BK)   For *any* p, *believe that* p *only if, for all you know,* p *(is true)*

I want to claim that (BK) is the constitutive norm of belief, and in so far as beliefs aim at knowledge, it is also a norm of knowledge. Since knowledge implies truth, (BK) is also the norm of truth. For assertion we have the corresponding norm (AK) above (§3.5): *Assert that* p *only if you know that* p. But one should be careful here. It is often said that truth is a normative concept. If this means that the fact that a proposition or belief is true implies that we have certain obligations, especially the obligation to believe it, then truth is certainly not "normative" in itself. For it would amount to (2), which, as we have seen, is just false. Similarly, a number of "ought" statements seem to be derivable from indicative ones, such as

(3) If your mother is ill, then you ought to visit her
(4) If it rains, you should take your umbrella

But as Allan Gibbard has remarked, it certainly does not make the concepts of *illness* or of *rain* "normative" (Gibbard forthcoming). They are normative only if other norms are presupposed, such as, for instance the norm that we should visit our parents when they are ill, or that we should try not to get wet, and so on. A familiar principle of the logic of obligation (deontic logic) is that one can derive an *ought* from an *is* in a conditional like (3) or (4) only if there is an *ought* in the antecedent. It is the same with truth, when "true" occurs in formulas such as (BK). *Truth is normative only in so far as there are norms for belief formation*. We could say, in philosophical jargon, that the norm of truth is supervenient, or dependent, upon the norm for belief and knowledge, but it is simpler to say that they are intrinsically interrelated. Now belief and knowledge are normative notions, and truth is normative in so far as it inherits its normativity from them. But in itself truth is not normative. There may be propositions that we do not believe or know, or even that no one can ever know, and that are true nevertheless. Norms only enter the picture when human activity comes in. As we saw, belief and knowledge imply standards of correctness and reasonableness, which are normative notions. In this sense, there is no norm of truth, but a norm of belief and knowledge. In other words, our *concept* of truth, in so far as it is related to those of belief and knowledge, is normative. But *truth-aptness* is not. This, however, might not calm certain worries that a number of philosophers have expressed concerning such claims about the normativity of truth. To say that it is a constitutive norm is to say that it is integral to our concepts of belief and knowledge that they aim at truth. It is a conceptual or logical, or, if one wants, an analytic or *a priori* connection. Such norms are conceptual norms.[4] But what has this to do with obligation, duty or value, which are, as we have seen, usually attached to the notion of norm? If there is a norm of truth in this conceptual sense, why should it be obligatory, or even desirable, to follow it? Are there other norms than the norm of truth, and if so what would be their relation to it? In other words, is this norm exhaustive and is it exclusive? In order to answer these questions, we have to answer another one: to be obliged to φ, in the usual sense, implies (a) that it is possible to φ, (b) that one is free to φ, which implies in turn (c) that one can will to φ. In other words, something is a norm only if we can comply with it by performing certain sorts of actions, or be sanctioned for not having performed them. Now, if truth is a norm for belief in *this* sense, it is quite distinct from the analytical or conceptual sense. There are, however, relations between the two, which we need to explore briefly.

5.2 The ethics of belief

Something is a norm, or a concept is normative, if it involves some sort of *evaluation* or appraisal, or some standard of correctness. In this sense, belief and knowledge are normative, and truth is, together with warrant, the appropriate dimension of appraisal. But the question just raised asks whether truth can be evaluative in a stronger sense. It is in fact not a question about what the conceptual norm is, but about whether it is itself valuable, desirable or dutiful. When we think of norms in this sense, we think most of the time of *practical* norms, that is, of norms for *actions*. And in general our normative vocabulary is divided into two different kinds of concepts:

(a) normative concepts of the *deontic* kind (sometimes referred to as normative concepts proper) such as "ought", "must", "should", "obligation", "requirement", "permission", "interdiction" "correctness", and so on. These are usually cashed in imperative terms and call for certain kinds of *actions* conforming to them.

(b) evaluative or *value* concepts proper, such as "good", "valuable", "desirable", "bad", "worth", and so on. These are usually cashed in terms of judgements, and the appropriate responses are not actions, but certain feelings or attitudes.

Which is the more fundamental? A familiar problem in meta-ethics is whether norms of the deontic kind can be reduced to values or the contrary. Here I shall leave out this question, and shall suppose that the kind of normative vocabulary that truth and belief can be related to will be either of kind (a) or of kind (b), but I shall refer mostly to concepts of kind (a). I also leave out for the moment the question whether we should be cognitivists or non-cognitivists about the nature of these norms. I shall just assume, in minimalist fashion, that the normative judgements involving them are at least *prima facie* truth-apt. Now we need another distinction, between:

(1) *practical* norms about what we should (ought to, etc.) *do*
(2) *epistemic* or *cognitive* norms about what we should *believe*[5]

Since (BT) and (BK) are about epistemic or cognitive attitudes, it seems clear that they refer to type (2) norms, and not to type (1) practical norms. But precisely, the claim that these could be norms in the (a) deontic sense implies that the proper responses to them should be actions. So the question is whether epistemic norms could, in some sense, be like practical norms, or involve some element of action. Now there is a thesis, which we have already met in §1.5, which closely ties belief to action, cognition to practice, hence epistemic norms or values to practical norms or values. This thesis is pragmatism. The question whether there are some obligations in the epistemic and/or the practical domain is the question of the "ethics of belief", and pragmatism is one answer to it. It is easy to see its link with the question of truth: for if truth is the norm of belief, we can also ask: is there an *ethics of truth*?

The "ethics of belief debate" goes back at least to the seventeenth century and to Locke, Hume, and other enlightenment writers who were interested in whether proof or evidence is the only criterion for good believing, or whether other forms of evaluation of belief, such as will or desire for the good, were possible (see Woltersdorff 1996, Owens 2000).[6] The writers, who, like Locke and Hume, hold that belief is ruled by the norm of evidence or warrant, and is not a matter of the will, are called *evidentialists*, and the writers who oppose them are called *voluntarists*.[7] The contemporary form of the debate set James in his famous lecture "The Will to Believe" (1897) against the Victorian scientist William Clifford who, in his essay "The Ethics of Belief" (1878), stated his famous evidentialist motto: "It is wrong, always, and everywhere, to believe anything on the basis of insufficient evidence." James replied, embracing a form of voluntarism, that it is sometimes good to believe things that are not evidentially warranted. There are many strands in this debate, but let us try to abstract from them, and to formulate what sets the evidentialist against the voluntarist.

Basically, these are opposed on what is itself a normative claim. The evidentialist denies, and the voluntarist affirms, that we ought to, or at least may, believe for other reasons than evidential epistemic reasons, that is, for pragmatic reasons. But to say that we ought to, or may, believe for non-evidential reasons, implies, according to the conditions (a)–(c) at the end of §5.1, that it is at least *possible* to believe in this way, and to be free to do it. But *ought* or *may* (normally) imply *can*. I can incur no obligation, or no permission, to do what it is impossible for me to do. So the normative claim put forward by the voluntarist implies the truth of a factual claim, namely that we *can* believe at will, or that it is a psychological possibility. So we can take the voluntarist to reject the following argument (which is therefore an antivoluntarist argument):

1. If normative deontological judgements about beliefs are true, belief is under the control of the will
2. Belief is not under the control of the will
3. Hence normative deontological judgements about beliefs are not true[8]

If premise (2) is false, the conclusion does not follow, and voluntarism is true. But it is not as simple as that. For certainly the evidentialist accepts the truth of at least this normative claim: we *ought* to believe on the basis of sufficient evidence. So it seems that the evidentialist's acceptance of (2) does not affect the conclusion (3). It is better to construct the evidentialist's claim as the claim that there is *no other norm* than the evidential norm of believing with sufficient evidence.[9] On the contrary, the voluntarist says that there might be other norms, practical ones, which might compete with, and possibly outrun, this epistemic norm.

But premise (2) in the antivoluntarist argument is, *prima facie*, true. Belief is not normally under the control of the will. I cannot decide to believe that p as the result of an intention to believe that p, which would result immediately in an action, in the way in which I can intend to go for a walk, and perform the action of walking. Not only does this seem psychologically impossible, but it is also conceptually impossible: given that beliefs aim at truth, to intend to believe that p at will, and to succeed in doing the resulting action, would imply that I could think of myself both as believing that *not p* (I cannot want to believe that p if I already believe p) and, as a result of my purported action, as believing that p.[10] So *direct* psychological voluntarism about belief is false. But this does not detract from the fact that we can have an *indirect* voluntary control on many of our beliefs, by manipulating the states in us that are involuntary and that we know to lead to certain beliefs. Hypnosis, autosuggestion, drugs, and other more exotic kinds of belief formation are certainly possible, and are as much the results of intentions as certain kinds of actions that do not count as "basic", such as moving one's leg or signalling for a turn. Many of such belief formations are irrational, but there is no reason why this should be necessary: attention, deliberation, weighing the evidence, or the conscious following of what Descartes called "rules for the direction of the mind" are modes of rational and voluntary indirect belief formation. So, after all, in *this* sense, premise (2) is false.

But does that license the pragmatist thesis that there can be good *practical* reasons to believe something at will, which could override our epistemic reasons, or even be our *only* reasons to believe? No. Concerning the first possibility – practical reasons taking precedence over epistemic ones – as we have just seen, there can certainly be cases of belief formation where considerations about the utility of a belief override considerations about how much evidence one has for it. But if belief is supposed to be in some sense an action, any action must take into account the truth of some beliefs about its consequences or the truth of some instrumental beliefs about its realization; hence practical reasons presuppose epistemic reasons, and cannot override them. Moreover, however desirable a belief can be, if there is little or no evidence for its truth, it remains irrational for this very reason. Most of the time it is because subjects are aware of the epistemic irrationality of their beliefs that they attend to considerations about their usefulness, and weigh the latter against the former. As we remarked above (§1.5) it is not because beliefs are useful that they are true (rational, justified), but because they are true that they can be useful. The same line of argument militates against the second possibility: that we could form beliefs at will *only* on the basis of practical considerations. Either these would have to be informed by evidentially constrained beliefs about their utility, or this would be to act, so to say, *blindly*, which can hardly be a good recipe for rationality. This is why Peirce called James's doctrine of the will to believe "suicidal".[11]

What is correct, however, in pragmatism, is the insistence on the fact that we might sometimes accept, or take for granted, certain beliefs for which we do not at present have sufficient evidence, and that we use as cornerstones for the formation of other beliefs. In this sense, scientists can accept a hypothesis that they are somewhat uncertain about, but which they have good reasons to hope to confirm later, or they can refuse to withdraw a theory that has proved to be cognitively fruitful, even though it is strongly threatened by counterevidence. But such voluntary activities belong to the course of deliberation for the sake of a theoretical activity, and they are means towards an end which is still that of epistemic justification and of search for truth.

This detour through the problems of the ethics of belief shows that there is no sense in which the norm of truth and knowledge can be understood as being intrinsically a practical norm, or to be dominated by practical norms. So it is fundamentally an epistemic norm, which cannot be reduced to another. The "ought" that figures in (BT) and (BK) is not, basically, an "ought" that refers to any *practical* obligation or responsibility that we have towards our beliefs as kinds of actions. Neither is it an "ought" that refers directly to an *epistemic* obligation or responsibility towards our beliefs as epistemic states.[12] It is, rather, "a *role* ought", of the kind that we express when we say, for instance

- "You ought to be walking in two weeks" (said by a physician to a patient)
- "You ought to see double" (said by a psychologist to a subject in an experiment on perception)   (Feldman 2000: 675)

Such "oughts" do not describe any obligation, and do not imply any sort of will, on the part of the subject, to conform to it. What they describe is the normal function, or the good performance, of certain states. Even when we say such things as "politicians ought to be honest", this does not necessarily refer to any subjective obligation on their part, but to the normal performance of a certain role.

I have said that truth is a functional concept (§3.3). It is part of this concept that such principles as (BT) or (BK) indicate its function. In this sense, again, there is nothing "normative", in the deontic sense, in these conceptual norms, and they do not presuppose any kind of voluntariness. It does not follow, however, that there is no relationship between these conceptual norms and the *further* obligations that we incur in the epistemic domain. We are not simply unreflective believers or knowers. We can be, and most often are, conscious of such norms as (BT) and (BK), and they govern our practice of believing and knowing. By attending to them in the course of an enquiry, we gain a reflective grasp of them, and we deliberate on the basis of them. This is a form of activity, which can involve decisions, intermediary steps and revisions. It can also involve stages where we balance epistemic and other, possibly practical, considerations about rationality in general. So the norm of truth and knowledge is the very foundation on which these other activities, which are guided by further norms, rest. We can now understand why the phrase "beliefs aim at truth" is so ambiguous. In so far as truth is the internal object of belief, and that belief cannot be the object of our will, "aiming at truth" is not a goal-directed activity, and it is wrong to say that truth is, in this teleological sense, the "goal of enquiry". But in so far as we become conscious of this norm in our knowing activities, we can reflect upon the role played by truth, and make it an aim in a teleological sense. To sum up, one can agree with Heal (1987) "that there is no goddess, Truth, of whom we might regard ourselves as priests or devotees", for it is false that we should know all truths, or that knowing the truth is automatically a Good Thing. But it does not follow that we cannot confer a specific *epistemic* value to truth. It is the *function* of beliefs to be directed towards truth, and we can become self-conscious of this function. But if the foregoing is correct, it does not make truth less normative for that.[13]

5.3 Cognitive suicide

Many philosophers suspect that such phrases as "the norm of truth" smuggle in the idea that there is some sort of intrinsic obligation or value to seek after truth. If what precedes is correct, one can agree with them that there is no such intrinsic obligation, but given that it is integral to the normal role of belief and knowledge that we ought to believe what is true, there is something self-defeating in the claim that we could turn our backs on this function, and to suggest that the enterprise of knowledge and enquiry could be led by following other norms, or no norm at all. But writers like Rorty do not find this self-defeating. On the contrary, they consider it as the only sensible view to take. According to Rorty, it is the essence of a sane "pragmatist" point of view:

> [Inquiry] has many different goals, none of which has metaphysical presupposition: getting what we want, the improvement of man's estate, convincing as many audiences as possible, solving as many problems as possible, and so on . . . This means that there is an obvious advantage in dropping the idea of a distinct goal or norm called "truth" – the goal of scientific inquiry, but not, for instance, of carpentry.
>
> (Rorty 1995: 297–8, 299)

But, contrary to what Rorty claims, it is one thing to ask whether scientific enquiry or theoretical life is, as Aristotle would say, the ultimate good, and to wonder why one should live the life of a scientist rather than the life of a carpenter. And it is another thing to suggest that enquiry might conform itself to other goals than knowledge, such as "getting what we want". If getting what we want turns out to be easier and more profitable if we engage in wishful thinking or self-deception or in various practices of "believing at will", then it seems to follow that there is, according to Rorty, nothing wrong in engaging in such practices. We might ask further whether, in the field of values in general, it is possible to engage in wishful thinking about what is right itself, that is, pursuing, in the field of enquiry, goals that are consciously opposed to truthfulness (B. Williams 1996: 25). For instance, why not side with creativity, or with other aesthetic values? Rorty's pluralism about goals is here based on his deflationism about truth. He claims to be a "pragmatist", but he does not say, unlike in other forms of pragmatism, that truth can be defined or reduced to utility. He wants to say that we cannot attach any intrinsic value to truth because there is nothing that we can intrinsically desire.

At this point, a question that we have raised above arises. It is the question whether we should be expressivists or cognitivists about the value of truth. Rorty is here clearly an expressivist: he claims that our values are supervenient upon our desires and attitudes, and have no objective status. Given that truth is, on the deflationist view, only a "compliment" that we pay to our favourite beliefs, the value of truth is only the *expression* of this complimentary attitude, and there as many ways of complimenting (valuing) our beliefs as one might imagine, all compatible with the innocuous use of the word "true" to label them. But apart from the problem that we have already dealt with – of how it is possible to reconcile an expressivist conception of value with a deflationist conception of truth – the objections that we have addressed to deflationism and our recognition of an objective norm of truth and knowledge lead us to adopt a *cognitivist* conception of the value or the norm of truth. This cognitivist conception follows from our claim that this norm, along with others, is intrinsically attached to belief. The norm (BT) is not the only one in play. There are other norms that depend upon it, such as the norm of *consistency* within beliefs, which belong to the class of logical norms. For instance, if someone believes that p, and that *if p then q*, then that person *ought* to believe that q. Now if this requirement or norm were not objective, if there were not such a thing as actually satisfying this constraint on belief, as an expressivist about norms wants to say, then it follows that we have no beliefs at all (Jackson 2000: 102).[14] This is certainly a strange conclusion but, on reflection, it is quite consistent with Rorty's "pragmatist" deflationism: there are no intrinsically cognitive attitudes that have the role of representing reality. Rorty's pragmatist eschews "unpragmatic questions such as: 'subjective or objective?', 'made or found', '*ad nos* or *in se*?'", and hopes that one day our culture will be replaced by a culture in which there would be no concern for truth (Rorty 1995: 290).[15]

There is, however, on the deflationist side, a more subtle line of criticism of the idea of the essential normativity of truth, which has been given by Paul Horwich. He does not deny that truth is a normative notion, nor that it is desirable. He accepts, to a large extent, that the norms (BT) or (BK) are in place. But he denies that these norms are intrinsic, for he holds that they can be explained in completely *non-normative* and purely descriptive terms. It is enough, according to him, that there exists a regular connection between our true beliefs and successful actions: it is the ordinary connection that exists between the things that we desire and our true instrumental beliefs about the actions that will lead to the fulfilment of these desires. This connection, says Horwich, explains why we want all of our beliefs to be true (Horwich 1990: 65).[16] Hence the value of truth is explained by the pragmatic value of the consequences of having true beliefs. What Horwich proposes, therefore, is a reduction of norm to value, and in turn a reduction of value to fact. But such an account faces three kinds of objections. The most obvious is that it seems to deny the fact that there can be, sometimes at least, a disinterested search for truth. Someone who holds that there are intrinsic values, things that are valued for their own sake, cannot accept Horwich's view.[17] But this is not an objection that follows from what I said above. The arguments that I have adduced in favour of the reality and intrinsicality of the norm of truth do not trade upon the notion of intrinsic *value*. They are actually neutral upon the ontological question of the reduction of norms to values. In that respect Horwich's view is a perfectly viable option. The second objection is that the purported "explanation" or "reduction" of the norm of truth proposed by Horwich does not square well with his deflationism, for if the value of truth is a property, which can be reduced to the utility of our true beliefs, it will be a substantive property, contrary to what deflationism claims. For the fact that truth can be desirable because it leads to successful actions is not, presumably, a superficial feature of it. The third objection is, I think, the most decisive. Horwich claims that we can translate normative epistemic terms such as "ought to believe", into purely descriptive terms such as "generally lead to practical benefits". But this leaves out the fact that there is something *right* with the having of true beliefs. Similarly one could suggest that we could translate the rule that if someone believes that p, and believes that *if p then q*, then one ought to believe that q, into a purely descriptive fact: if someone does not believe that q in such a case, that person fails to believe an obvious consequence of the belief. This leaves out the fact that in such a case the person is *wrong* to fail to believe this. This is not to say that there cannot be any reductive account of normative language in descriptive terms, but that if there is such an account it must try to meet the claims of normative language *in their own terms*, that is, without changing the subject.[18] When we formulate the norm of truth as "believe what is true", what we say is that there are good *reasons* to do so (and it is why the formulation of this norm is not (2) of §5.1 above, but (BT) or (BK)). If the norm of truth is also a norm of knowledge, Horwich's descriptive translation fails to account for the normativity that is present in the notion of knowledge too. This purported translation also suggests that our good reasons might be practical reasons, hence that the rationality of our beliefs could depend only upon our attending their practical consequences. But as we have seen, in our discussion of the ethics of belief, this is false.

In the last resort, the only way to avoid these problems would be just to deny that there are any epistemic norms at all. This would mean denying not only that our beliefs obey any normative constraints, but also that there could be any way in which our cognitive systems could evolve beneficially (through evolution or otherwise), or that there could be any debate about this. This would mean accepting a form of *eliminativism* about rationality and normativity in general. Steven Stich (1990) takes such a view, and he also calls it "pragmatism". He denies that beliefs, if we take them to be psychological states related to semantic contents, can be mapped by a unique interpretation function onto states that would have a semantic evaluation as true or false. Moreover, there is, according to Stich, no uniquely good system of cognitive processes – such as those that would be true or rational – which would lead to optimal results. Hence there are no such things as beliefs, truth, or rationality. But, like eliminativism about mental states, when it says that we do not have any beliefs, desires, intentions, and so on, this fails to explain the most obvious facts about the way we conceive ourselves. This kind of normative blindness, as we might call it, may appear, like Rorty's pragmatism, as a healthy liberation from tenacious illusions and supersitions. But it also looks like a form of cognitive suicide.

5.4 What's wrong with relativism

I have been much concerned here with a view of truth that typically deflates the idea that truth has a normative significance, as well as any attempt to theorize about it. This view was quite alien to the founders of the pragmatic movement, who cared a lot about the "meaning of truth" and wanted to replace, rather than eliminate, our theoretical ideals within the overall scheme of human life and society. Not all deflationists are moved by a desire to downgrade our best theoretical efforts; what they suggest, rather, is that we can continue these efforts without trying to solve the apparently deep issues about truth.[19] But the fact is that, today, pragmatism often means, as Simon Blackburn has remarked:

> The denial of differences, the celebration of the seamless web of language, the soothing away of distinctions, whether of primary versus secondary qualities, fact *versus* value, description *versus* expression, of any other significant kind. What is left is a smooth, undifferentiated view of language, sometimes a nuanced kind of anthropomorphism or "internal" realism, sometimes the view that has no view is possible: minimalism, deflationism, quietism. (Blackburn 1998a: 157)

If this is "pragmatism", then I have argued that we should not be pragmatists. There is, however, a more traditional way of reaching such a "don't care" attitude of tolerance about theoretical matters, and it lurks behind many of these views. It is relativism. It is the doctrine that at least some, and possibly all, truths are relative to contexts, persons, communities, cultures, perspectives, or conceptual schemes. There is a sense in which the claim that truth is relative to contexts is quite correct. This is especially the case for the utterance of indexical sentences ("I am here"), tense sentences ("He loved her"), but also sentences that contain relative words ("He is tall": he might be a tall pygmy, but quite short by other standards). Such utterances may fail to express the same proposition depending on the circumstances. But the context sensitivity of most sentences that are not, as Quine calls them, "eternal", such as "2 + 2 = 4" or "Napoleon invaded Russia", does not show these cannot be true or false when we fix the relevant parameters. Once I understand "I am here" as being about Pascal Engel and about my being in Paris, the truth does not become "relative" to me and to Paris. If I can understand this, it shows that there is some stable meaning that allows me to state the truth conditions of "I am here." Neither is relativism objectionable if it is the thesis that every truth is relative to a representation, or that different people may judge differently. For they can do so, without this entailing that there is no absolute truth transcending their perspectives. The latter is the distinctive relativist thesis. The best way to formulate it is to note that for the relativist, two statements that contradict each other can both be true if they are made from a different perspective or point of view. Hence the following situation is possible:

(1) p (relative to *my* system, say S1)
(2) *not p* (relative to *yours*, say S2)
(3) hence: p_{S1} *and not* p_{S2} is true

But this claim is incoherent. For the very statement that p_{S1} *and not* p_{S2} can be true must itself be true relative to some system: p_{S1} *and not* p_{S2} *(relative to* S1*)*. So relativism cannot even be stated. This is a version of Plato's classical objection to Protagoras (in the *Theaetetus*) or of Aristotle's objections to the Sophists in book Γ of the *Metaphysics*. To this the relativist can of course answer that it is improper to conjoin p and *not p* when they are true in different systems, and thus reject (3). But suppose p is the statement that relativism is true. Then *not p* will be the claim that relativism is false. But if relativism is true, this claim *not p* can only be true relative to another system than relativism, presumably from the point of view of the absolutist. But if the thesis that *relativism is false* can be true from another perspective, relativism will be true only from its own perspective. Not a very satisfying result. A second objection concerns the meaning of p and *not p*, when it is said, in the manner of (3), that they can be contradictory, but nevertheless both true with respect to each system. The very possibility of saying this supposes that we can understand these sentences and what they mean. But if their meaning depends upon their truth conditions, there must be something common to the two sentences, namely these truth conditions, and if these can be invariant, truth itself cannot vary so radically from context to context. Relativists can extend their view to a view about meaning, and say that meaning itself varies according to perspective (this is often what the doctrine known as "conceptual relativism" or the meaning variance of statements according to "paradigms", "schemes", etc. amounts to). But if there is a systematic variation of meaning in p, then p_{S1} *and not* p_{S2} cannot even be asserted.[20] A third and related objection is that relativism cannot be stated if it amounts to the thesis that

(4) p is true relative to a person P or a community C iff P or C *believes p*.

But the fact that P or C believes p is either a relative affair (they believe p by their own lights, so to speak), or it isn't. If it isn't then there is no way to formulate the proposed condition. And if it is, then there is at least one absolute truth about what P or C believes.[21] I do not intend to say that these objections are knock-down, and that this is the end of the matter. But they all turn upon the self-defeating character of the doctrine, which is well expressed by Putnam's well-known expression of it: "Relativism is true (for me)."

Weaker forms of relativism, however, might be countenanced. Sometimes it is formulated as the view that there are many true descriptions of the world, couched in many different vocabularies. Or we could say that there are many "conceptual schemes". If this means that compatible distinct descriptions exist, this is correct, but if this means that truth is itself relative to such schemes, and that there can be two alternative conceptual schemes that are incompatible but true, then the view falls into the incoherence just noted. As I have already pointed out (§3.4) Michael Lynch (1998) has defended a conception of truth that has strong affinities with the minimal realism presented here. But he holds also that our very notions of fact and content are relative to conceptual schemes, and that this licenses a form of "pluralism", which is compatible with a realist conception of truth, hence does not entail a relativism about *truth*. Now if "pluralism" means, like the functionalist conception of truth defended above (§3.3), that truth will not be realized in the same way in every domain, this is correct. This is a *conceptual* pluralism. But if this means, as Lynch actually suggests, a *metaphysical* pluralism, according to which there are many totally independent and incompatible regions of reality, such a kind of pluralism is not an implication of minimal realism as I have defended it here. MR allows that the realist/anti-realist issues will not present themselves in the same way in various domains, but it does not say that the domains will be irreducible to each other, and that there will be no communication and no dependence between the "realities" in, say, ethics and natural science, or natural science and psychology. For instance, it does not say that science investigates the natural properties of things, but ethics the "non-natural" properties. Realism implies that there is a "shared world" beyond the conceptual schemes, although it accepts that the question of the objectivity in various domains is not uniform.[22]

The best way to see what is wrong with strong relativism is to consider its application within the set of views that are called "postmodernist", the consequences of which have been so well revealed in various recent episodes in the intellectual scene such as the famous "Sokal affair". In order to ridicule the doctrines and practices of some circles in what is known as "science studies", the physicist Alan Sokal sent a text for publication in the journal *Social Text*, called "Transgressing the Boundaries: Toward a Transformative Hermeutics of Quantum Gravity". The text was a parody of relativist talk and of the current practice in these circles of using ill-understood or meaningless fashionable scientific terms to promote the view that science is a "constructed" social phenomenon. Although obviously ridiculous, the text was accepted and published. This meant, according to Sokal, that the editors of the journal readily applied their relativistic doctrine, for they could not tell the difference between a parody and serious scholarship. Recently a similar episode (but with no hoax) happened on the French academic scene, when a famous astrologist was awarded a doctorate in sociology at the Sorbonne, which defended the view that astrology has equal credentials with astronomy as a "serious" science.

In general such people reply to their critics on the basis of the relativistic view that science is just one of the ways of knowing the world, and that it is an offence to tolerance to say that unrestricted metaphorical gossip, astrology or loose sociology do not have an equal entitlement to be true as "serious" science and scholarship (of course, the French intellectuals attacked by Sokal replied on similar pluralistic "grounds"). Now suppose that one holds the view that astrology has equal claims to truth with astronomy. Since they contradict each other, the defender of astrology has to say that they are both true ((3) above). But that only means (according to (4)) that the friend of astrology believes that astrology is true, and the foe believes that it is not. But then the view can be applied to itself. If there is a perspective from which both are right, then there is a perspective from which both *cannot* be right. Relativists, being tolerant of all views, must be tolerant of this one. But they cannot be, unless they undermine their own view. The same reasoning holds if we do not talk in terms of truth, but in terms of epistemic standards or rules of evidence. The friends of astrology have to say that their own epistemic standards are as justified as those of their adversaries. The same argument as the one with truth then applies.[23] And of course the argument applies to any relativist view of normative standards. The only option left to relativists seems to be to avoid asserting their own view, and to appeal, like the traditional sceptics, to suspension of judgement, or like Rorty, to irony, deconstruction, or to the claim that they are telling another "story" than the traditional one, or proposing another "vocabulary": "truth does not belong to my vocabulary". Perhaps what the relativist wants to say is that it is a mistake to impose equally stringent standards on truth in matters, such as science and mathematics, where objective truth does seem to make sense, and to other matters, such as ethics, politics or fiction, where we can perhaps hope for less. But if relativists pretend to renounce truth in these matters, *and* to defend a uniform view about truth – even if it is a "no-theory" theory of truth – it is hard to see how they can keep the possibility of talking of truth in the "harder" disciplines. Conversely, as Bernard Williams remarks, when people have invoked the values of truth and truthfulness in political matters, their natural paradigm was not that of preserving truth about ethics or politics: they wanted to preserve the capacity for talk of truth in other matters. As Orwell said in *1984*: "Freedom is the freedom to say that twice two is four" (Williams 1996: 25). If we can't be truthful in politics, where less than truth is to be expected, how can we be truthful in science, where more is to be expected?

Conclusion: Truth regained

The question from which we started was: can truth be defined? In Chapter 1, we departed from the substantive theories that give a positive answer to this question. In Chapter 2 we resisted the deflationist move that attempts to empty truth of any substance. In Chapters 3 and 4, we took the minimal realist line that allows our concept of truth to keep slim, without preventing us from accepting realism about truth-aptness. This led us to a reinflation, or resubstantialization, of the concept of truth and of the property that it denotes. But the "substance" that was thus reintroduced is not the substance that was aimed at by the definitional attempts of traditional theories. Truth has substance because it is constitutively linked to belief, assertion and knowledge and because it is a normative property of our knowledge-seeking enquiries. Truth in this sense is indefinable because it is a concept that cannot be analysed except from its relations with these other concepts. I concur in this respect with Davidson when he says:

> For the most part the concepts philosophers single out for attention, like truth, knowledge, belief, action, cause, the good and the right, are the most elementary concepts without which (I am inclined to say) we would have no concepts at all. Why then should we be able to reduce these concepts definitionally to other concepts that are simpler, clearer, and more basic?
> (Davidson [1995] 1999: 309)[1]

In a sense, a deflationist could agree with this. But such a non-reductionist view does not imply that when we attempt to analyse truth through its connections with other notions, such as knowledge, meaning and belief, nothing of substance is achieved, and that we do not need to say anything about the nature of these concepts and their interrelations. Finding a place for truth, and other semantic properties, within the other properties and entities that compose the world is a theoretical enterprise, which cannot simply be disposed of by claiming that these are thin concepts. Analytic philosophy, at one stage of its evolution at least, has tended to isolate the analysis of such notions as truth, meaning, and content within the domain of a purely linguistic and conceptual investigation, and a number of contemporary conceptions of truth still bear the mark of this methodological turn. But the present analyses have not led us into that direction. On the contrary they have led us to consider the realist/anti-realist issues as being as substantive as they ever have been. In many ways, the theory of truth is a collection of truisms, but the very fact that one can disagree on the truisms shows that it is not *purely* a collection of truisms.

Among the main reasons why truth can regain substance from the deflationist washbasin[2] there is, as I have tried to show in Chapter 5, the fact that it has a normative status. This does not imply that Truth is a goddess of whom academics or scientists can regard themselves as priests or devotees, or that the "disinterested search for truth" is a kind of superstition.[3] It implies, however, that truth is a norm of knowledge and enquiry. There is no ethics of belief and enquiry that is directly built into the notion of truth, but it does not follow that there is no ethics of enquiry.

The overall assessment of the place of truth within the realm of values is a further question to which the present enquiry leads. I have not examined it here, but it is certainly one of the main issues that contemporary philosophy has to face. It is often said that, with the advent of the scientific image in the seventeenth century, the world has become, to use Max Weber's celebrated phrase, "disenchanted", and that our conception of reality has become one of a cold, value-free, description of what there is and of naked facts.[4] One of the contemporary philosophers who have, with Rorty, done most to defend a relativistic and nihilist conception of truth, Michel Foucault, locates in philosophy this disenchantment to the time of Descartes. With Descartes, Foucault says, "I can be immoral and know the truth" (Foucault 1997, quoted in Owens 2000: 177).[5]

Against this, Foucault, in his late writings, argued that we should come back to the ancient idea of spirituality and human flourishing, and that we should essentially search for a form of *practical* wisdom, which would promote philosophy as a non-theoretical enterprise. But there is a strong tension between this late Foucaldian emphasis on ethical values and what he has constantly claimed in his previous work: that we should renounce all talk of truth altogether, because truth is the instrument of power through science and technical progress. According to Foucault, truth can only be the object of a "history", like Nietzsche's history of an "error". This postmodernist claim about the historicity of the concept of truth, of which Foucault is one of the most flamboyant representatives,[6] stands in sharp contrast to G. E. Moore's (1901) claim that "There is, properly speaking, no history of the terms ["true" and "false"] since they have always been used in philosophy and always in very much the same sense." Although there is a history of the representations and of the social *attitudes* that we have taken towards it (including, as Foucault emphasized, of our *desire* for truth), and a history of our philosophical conceptions of truth, there is no history of truth *as such*. If truth, as I have argued, has a core minimal realist sense, this sense is not time-relative, nor context-relative.

It should be clear that in this book I have stood up for Moore, and rejected the Foucaldian thesis and its relativistic or sceptical variants. The late Foucault came to regret the modernist divorce between epistemic norms and ethical norms that followed the advent of modern science, and reverted to an "ethics of the self" that would renew the ancient quest for spirituality. But Foucault did not see that his own eliminativism about truth did little to attenuate the divorce. He satisfied himself with the opposition between cold science, supposedly devoted to flat truth, and the healthy practice of "caring for oneself", but he failed to see that knowledge and the epistemic realm was also liable to values, because he considered knowledge as a mere instrument of power. Contrary to this, as I have suggested, an investigation into the connections between ethical and cognitive values should lead us to put truth back into the whole picture.

Notes

Introduction

1. A characteristic statement of the postmodernist view is Allen (1993). For such comparisons between "Continental" and "analytic" treatments, see Engel (1997, 1999c).

Chapter 1: Classical theories of truth

1. I should perhaps say "most languages", for I do not consider whether there are any human languages that do not have such a predicate. But all have a word to that effect.
2. The figure is inspired by Wright (1999).
3. On the distinction between definition of truth and criteria for truth, see Russell (1966).
4. For an excellent account of Aristotle on truth, see Crivelli (1996, 1999, and their references).
5. On the theory of truth as *adaequatio*, see Schultz (1993). Anselm, in *De Veritate* (1998) talks of *rectitudo*; the tradition has also *conformitas*.
6. Descartes (1964–76, II, 597, letter to Mersenne, 16 October 1639): "Truth is such a transcendentally clear notion that it is impossible to ignore it . . . one can explain it *quid nominis* to those who do not understand the language, and to say to them that this word, *truth*, in its proper meaning, denotes the conformity of thought to the object, when it is attributed to things which are outside the mind . . . but one cannot give any logical definition which might help to know its nature." See also Descartes (1964–76, VII, 37, VIII, 220); Leibniz (1705, IV, 5 §11; Hume ([1748] 1968: III, 1, p. 458); Kant ([1781] 1929: A58).
7. For instance Kant, in the passage cited in note 6, says that the "nominal definition" of truth is "the agreement of knowledge with its object". Leibniz, however, says that the kind of "*convenance*" between ideas and things which is concerned here is of "a very particular kind" (*op.cit.*).

8. The argument is spelled out by Blackburn (1985: 227–8). It does not originate with Frege. It can be found, for instance, in Gregory of Rimini (1522, Prologue, quaestio 1, art.1.)

9. On Aristotle's use of *"pragma"* see de Rijk (1987). On truth-makers, see Mulligan *et al.* (1984). The Aristotelian tradition called these truth-makers "accidents"; Husserl calls them "moments" (see Husserl 1901: III), others "tropes". (I prefer the spelling "truth-maker" to Armstrong's (2000) "truthmaker", since I do not want to assume that a theory of truth-making has necessarily to take the form that he gives to it.)

10. Moore also held such a view, and both he and Russell actually seem to have taken it from Bradley. See Baldwin (1991b).

11. See Prior (1971: 10). Frege balked at this when Russell said to him that Mont Blanc *itself*, with its snows and rocks, was a genuine constituent of the proposition *that Mont Blanc is 4000 m high*, cf. Frege (1979: 163). Frege would rather say that it is the *sense* of the word "Mont Blanc" that figures in the *sense* of the proposition, and that is the object of judgement, not the *referent*.

12. The argument was first formulated explicitly by Gödel, who based it on considerations drawn from Frege and Church. It was later elaborated by Quine and Davidson. See the latter's "True to the Facts", in Davidson (1984: 41–2); and for a general analysis, Neale (1995, 2001).

13. The point is also put by Strawson (1950) in terms of sentences: facts are individuated in terms of sentences.

14. See for instance Hale & Wright (1997: 427–57) and Alston (1996) on Putnam's argument, and Quine (1960) and Davidson, "The Inscrutability of Reference" (in Davidson 1984).

15. See Barwise & Perry (1983), Taylor (1976), Forbes (1986), Bennett (1988).

16. See in particular Mulligan *et al.* (1984) and B. Smith (1999).

17. Armstrong does not mention the slingshot argument. To allow the truth-makers to be less embracing, Armstrong has to distinguish other truth-makers that are part of this whole, and to define what he calls the minimal truth-maker for a particular truth (the one that makes it true, but that does not contain further truth-makers that are parts of it). See Armstrong (2000: 7).

18. Williamson (1999) shows that the principle TM contradicts a well-known and accepted principle of modal logic, the converse Barcan Formula: necessarily if everything is B then everything is necessarily B. Armstrong's position about negative states of affairs is not very clear. In his 1997 book, he rejects them (pp. 19, 135). But in Armstrong (2000), and in a personal communication, he countenances them. For a discussion of the truth-maker principle, cf. Moreland (2001: 26–7).

19. I am indebted here to David Armstrong and to Kevin Mulligan. One possibility would be to say that the truth-maker theory implies an *identity* theory of truth, in the sense below (§1.6). But if the relation between the world and truth is that of supervenience this suggestion is borne out.

20. The objection is Russell's ("On the Nature of Truth and Falsehood" (1910) in Russell 1966).
21. For Bradley's doctrine of degrees of truth, see Bradley (1914).
22. The example is Russell's ("Williams James' Conception of Truth", in Russell 1966).
23. For an excellent account of these differences, see Skorupski (1997a).
24. For an analysis of Fitch's argument, see Williamson (2000: Ch. 11). Its impact on Putnam's ideal verificationism is discussed by Wright (2000: 355–7). See also Tennant (1997: Ch. 8).
25. "William James' Conception of Truth" (1910) in Russell (1966).
26. See Whyte (1990) and Mellor (1991). The view is analysed in Dokic & Engel (2002).
27. See, for example, Millikan (1984) and Papineau (1987).
28. As Wright (2000) notes, there is often a misunderstanding of Peirce on this point. He does not actually say that truth is the ideal point on which inquirers *would* converge in ideal circumstances, but that it is the point where they *will* converge, and are "fated" to do so (*Collected Papers*, Vol. VIII: 139, Wright 2000: 336; see also Misak 1991).
29. For an analysis of Peirce's pragmatism as both idealism and realism see Tiercelin (1998).
30. See Baldwin (1991b), Dodd (1995, 2001), Hornsby (1998), Candlish (1999) and Engel (2001a). I have suggested that this view has some affinities with truth-maker realism. Haldane (1993) suggests that it is congenial to Thomistic metaphysics.
31. As Hornsby (1998) says, borrowing a phrase from McDowell (1994), who seems to defend a view of this kind (see below § 3.2), the truth-bearers are "thinkables".
32. As Baldwin (1990: 42–3) notes: "The resulting metaphysical system can seem almost idealist: the world is, quite literally, a world of meanings."
33. The trivial version of the identity theory comes, in many respects, close to the deflationary views that are examined in the next chapter. Hornsby's (1998) and perhaps McDowell's (1994) minimalist versions oscillate between the substantive and the minimalist concepts of truth, and in this sense they are ambiguous. See Dodd (2001) and Engel (2001a).

Chapter 2: Deflationism

1. The word "redundant" comes originally from W. E. Johnson's *Logic* (1920).There are, however, expressions of the transparency feature in Gregory of Rimini in the thirteenth century and in various medieval authors. Even Aristotle (*Metaphysics* Γ 7, 1011b 26) could in one sense be considered as an expression of it. For a review of the various deflationary and minimalist views on truth, see O'Leary Hawthorne & Oppy (1997).
2. This view is elaborated by C. J. F. Williams (1976), following Prior (1971), and to some extent Mackie's (1973) conception of "simple truth".

3. It was introduced by Prior (1971) and elaborated by Grover (1992) and Brandom (1994). Ramsey anticipated it (Ramsey 1991: 10).

4. Prior actually used "thether" see Prior (1971: 16–21); and, for a detailed analysis of such devices, Grover (1992) and Künne (forthcoming).

5. The traditional example is "Empedocles leaped" which is true (in English) of Empedocles falling into the volcano, but which is false (in German: *Empedocles liebt*), for (let us suppose) he did not love anybody.

6. See Field (1986, 1994).

7. On such difficulties, see David (1992: Ch. 5).

8. For presentations, see for instance Quine (1970), Engel (1991), Kirkham (1992) and Soames (1999).

9. There are others ways of dealing with the Liar paradox, which do not employ Tarski's hierarchy. See Kripke (1975) and Martin (1984).

10. For an illustration to such partial definitions, see Blackburn (1985) and Engel (1991).

11. Some readings of Tarski, however, take him as a physicalist, who attempted to define truth in more primitive terms, and Field (1972) has argued that this could serve as a basis for a causal account of truth and reference.

12. Field (1994) insists on these differences.

13. Of course "and" is here defined through truth, in which case a deflation-ary account can be given of it too, but it can also be defined in terms of certain inference rules. Actually the deflationary analysis of "true" resem-bles the view that the meaning of logical words can be given through their associated rules of inference, without using the semantic notion of truth, but only the proof-theoretic apparatus. Horwich (1990: 77–9) addresses this issue; cf. Engel (1991).

14. "If we accept the redundancy theory of 'true' and 'false' ... the truth table explanation is quite unsatisfactory. In order that someone should gain from the explanation that P is true in such and such circumstances an understanding of the sense of P, he must already know what it means to say that P is true. If when he inquires into this he is told that the only explanation is that to say that P is true is the same as to assert P, it will follow that in order to understand what is meant by saying that P is true he must already know the sense of asserting P, which was precisely what was supposed to be explained to him" (Dummett [1959] 1978: 7, see also Wittgenstein, *Tractatus* 4.1).

15. H. Field (1986, 1994) has suggested an account of meaning that might supplement his deflationary conception: meaning is conceptual role. This has to be a different view from Horwich's, though, since Field claims that deflationary truth is a property that a sentence has independently of the way the sentence is used by speakers (1986: 58).

16. See, for instance, Dummett ([1959] 1978: 6–7).

17. On the medieval use of "transcendental", see for example Kenny & Pinborg (1982: 493). I am not suggesting, however, that the scholastics treated "true" as not being a genuine property of propositions, but that their emphasis on the generality of *verum*, and the fact that it is not a

property like the others, points towards a feature that the contemporary deflationist views have rediscovered.

18. See, for instance, McDowell (1981, 1987, 1994) and §3.2.
19. Bolzano, *Paradoxes of the Infinite*, §13, *Wissenschafstlehre*, I: 147. I owe these references to Wolfgang Künne (forthcoming).
20. On "deferential beliefs", see Récanati (2000).
21. On Moore's paradox see Moore (1993: 207 ff.) and Goldstein (2000) for a Wittgensteinian analysis.
22. It violates, as Wittgenstein says, the "logic of assertion", although it is not a logical contradiction.
23. The notion of "direction of fit" is from Anscombe (1958); "aiming at truth" comes from B. Williams (1970).
24. Note that this difficulty is not unrelated to the difficulty that the redundantist view encounters with "blind" ascriptions: the very fact that we cannot group together truth-ascriptions of the form "What he says is true" is closely related to the fact that truth, on this view, becomes a distinct predicate attached to each assertion. Assertion, and not truth, is what is common to each particular occurrence of "It is true that *p.*"
25. Horwich (1990: 87–8) addresses this point, but he does not say anything satisfactory. See Chapter 3.
26. See, for example, Derrida (1982).
27. Haack (1993, 1998) has a proper label for Rorty's kind of pragmatism: she calls it "Vulgar Pragmatism", especially in contrast to Peirce's pragmatism.
28. See *The Gay Science*, §373. quoted in A. W. Moore (1997: 104). Nietzsche has some Rortyan deflationists accents when he writes "Agreeable opinion is agreed as true" (*Human, All Too Human,* I, §180).

Chapter 3: Minimal realism

1. See, for example, Dummett (1978, 1991, 1996).
2. Wright takes inspiration here from Wiggins's (1980) idea that there are "marks of truth". In other writings Wright includes among the platitudes the very syntactical features such as embedding. See, for example, Wright (1999).
3. Jackson et al. (1994: 291–2).
4. What Wiggins calls "marks" are not criteria for truth, but something closer to what Frege calls the *Merkmale*, the characterizing traits, of a concept.
5. Cf. M. Johnston (1993); Wright (1992: Ch. 4).
6. Putnam (1994) calls it a "recoil" phenomenon, where philosophers move back and forth between realism and anti-realism.
7. Putnam takes inspiration from Diamond (1996). The "realism" in question consists of rejecting all forms of philosophical realism or anti-realism. See Child (2000) against such readings.
8. Putnam comes close to acknowledging this (1994: 463 fn).

9. This has been read as an expression of the "identity theory of truth" (see the references in Ch. 1 note 30 above), perhaps as a deflationist version of it (see Ch. 1 note 33 above).

10. As Putnam reminds us, divorcing his own view from Reid's (Putnam 1994: 468).

11. See, for instance, J. J. Gibson's (1979) ecological approach to perception.

12. This line of thought is Wright's (2000). He in fact argues for his own version of ideal verificationism.

13. This was in fact Ramsey's lesson, when he said that there is no separate problem of truth, but a separate problem of what belief is. See §2.4.

14. See Shapiro (1998: 502).

15. Wright acknowledges the distinction between truth and truth-aptness, and the distinction between the corresponding minimalisms (1998: 185). But, as I point out below, he blurs this distinction, since he is a minimalist about truth-aptness too.

16. The functionalist suggestion is Pettit's (1996). It is taken up by Lynch (2001a).

17. I have myself defended a similar view under this very name, elsewhere, in Engel (1991: 74–9; 1994a: Ch. 5; 1998). But in these other attempts to formulate minimal realism, I had not insisted enough on the realist commitments of the view. (I am indebted to Susan Haack for pointing this out to me.)

18. I examine briefly Lynch's view, which came to my attention only when this manuscript was completed, below (§4.5) Other views that are close to the present one are Van Cleve (1996) and Sosa (1993).

19. Almeder (1992) defines "blind realism" as the view according to which our beliefs can correctly describe the external world, without our knowing which of our beliefs do describe it. S. Haack (1993, 1998: 156 ff.) defends a position that is close to Peirce's "critical commonsensism". Unlike Peirce's view, neither Haack's "innocent realism" nor MR are committed to a form of ideal limit conception of truth. MR comes especially close to Haack's views when she rejects a correspondence requirement for realism, and when she insists on the normativity of truth. See Chapter 5. (Thanks to Susan Haack on these points.)

20. This formulation is obviously inspired by Alston (1996: 7).

21. Philosophy teachers who grade papers are often surprised by how anti-realist and relativist the "common sense" of students is.

22. This distinction is roughly the one that Searle makes (1969) between "regulative" and "constitutive" rules. It is also explained by Wright (1992: 15–16).

23. This is Horwich's reaction. See Horwich (1996); see also the second edition of his *Truth* (1998b).

24. See, for instance, Frege (1979: 130).

25. Williamson recognizes this (2000: 243, fn 2, 1996: 908).

26. This implies an externalist conception of knowledge.

Chapter 4: The realist/anti-realist controversies

1. See, for instance, Putnam (1971, 1975: vol. 1, 74).
2. See, for example, Tennant (1987: Ch. 2) and Wright (1992: 5).
3. For relevant examples of discussion in these respective domains, see Lewis (1986, 1987), Stich (1982), Jackson (1986) and Dummett "The Reality of the Past" (in Dummet 1978).
4. See Dummett "Realism" (in Dummett 1981).
5. This is one of the reasons why we should pay attention to the distinction between truth and truth-aptness (cf. §3.3).
6. Hacking (1983) has defended a related view.
7. See Ramsey "General Propositions and Causality" (in Ramsey 1990: 145–63), Wittgenstein 1969 II, 15., Ryle (1950).
8. "Projectivism" is Blackburn's term (cf. Blackburn 1985: Ch. 6, 1992). See also §3.3.
9. See Rorty (1986) and Hesse's reply in the same volume. A sensible assessment of the dispute is given by Haack (1987, 1998: Ch. 4), who notes that Rorty has to deny that metaphors can express anything.
10. Davidson, "What Metaphors Mean" (in Davidson 1984).
11. Sometimes Horwich seems to be close to this position, but often he just says that his minimalism leaves the issues open.
12. One writer for whom this distinction counts is Van Fraassen (1981).
13. Psillos (1998: Ch. 10) has an excellent discussion of Fine's views.
14. Leaving aside Plato and Aristotle, G. E. Moore's *Principia Ethica* (1903) is the most famous view of the first kind, utilitarianism the most influential view of the second kind.
15. This is John Mackie's view (see Mackie 1977).
16. See especially Smith 1994a, for the most conspicuous treatment of this view.
17. The problem was described as "Frege's point" by Geach (1965). See Blackburn (1985: 189 ff.).
18. John Skorupski's *irrealist cognitivism* might also be a view of this kind (see Skorupski 2000).
19. This, I take it, is the line pursued by Michael Smith (1994b), in his book *The Moral Problem*, where he finally adopts a version of cognitivism.
20. Here again I am drawing on Wright's (1988) excellent survey.
21. I have, however, encountered the view held by some psychoanalysts. This is, of course, distinct from the thesis that mathematical objects are in some sense mental constructions, or even constructions out of our brains.
22. For a characteristic statement, see Wittgenstein (1956, II, 27, 28, reprinted in Blackburn & Simmons 1999: 11–112).
23. This is argued by Blackburn (1990).
24. On these issues, see Peacocke (1993) and Engel (1991).
25. See also the references in §2.2.
26. Wright (1983) attributes this view to Frege.
27. See Wright (1992: 149, 1998; Hale 1997: 293).
28. Davidson (1990) can be interpreted as saying just this. He hopes to explain the concept of truth by tying it to a whole network in his theory of interpretation.

29. A more precise development of this line of thought would have to go into the issues about vagueness that we haven't been able to treat here (see Williamson 1994a). It is also close to the idea expressed by Almeder's "blind realism". See Chapter 3, note 19.
30. See Van Cleve (1996: 874) and Sosa (1993) for similar views.
31. I take this framework to be very close to what Peacocke (1999: Ch. 1) calls "the integration challenge": "We have to reconcile a plausible account of what is involved in the truth of a statement of a given kind with a credible account of how we can know those statements when we do know them" (p. 1). Peacocke's programme implies that a "linking thesis" (Ch. 2) is true: concepts are in each domain individuated by their possession conditions.

Chapter 5: The norm of truth

1. See, for instance, Geach, "History of a Fallacy" (in Geach 1968).
2. The point is Williamson's (1994b: 134). Horwich (1998a: Ch. 7) has an answer to this, which is complex, but not really convincing. Moreover he does not take it as an argument against the idea that assertion and belief could be governed by a single norm. See below.
3. "Is true" is of course redundant, but I introduce it to make the connection between belief and truth explicit.
4. Peacocke (1992) calls such conceptual norms the "normative liaisons" of a concept.
5. As Skropuski (1997a) notes, there are also norms about what we should *feel*, which do not fall squarely within category (1) or (2), nor within (a) or (b). But I shall leave aside this important point here.
6. The debate of course goes back to the Middle Ages, when theologians asked whether faith or belief was a matter of the will.
7. Sometimes, Pascal, in his famous wager argument for the existence of God, is taken to be a voluntarist, but it is not clear (cf. Elster 1978).
8. I have adapted here Feldman's (2000) formulation of this argument (he actually proposes an antivoluntarism argument, in the form of a *modus tollens* denying the consequent of (1)).
9. As Haack (1997) remarks, this is obscured in the James–Clifford debate by the fact that they conflate epistemic justification with practical justification.
10. The classic argument to this effect is Williams (1970). It has many twists and turns, and has been contested. But I take it to be basically correct. See, for example, Winters (1979), Engel (1999a) and Noordhof (2001).
11. See Perry (1935: 438). See also D. Owens (2000: 29–31).
12. In this sense the norm of truth, as it is construed here, does not commit us to a *deontological theory of justification*, according to which to be justifed in believing that *p* is to satisfy certain deontic requirements.
13. I completely concur with Haack's "Confessions of an Old-fashioned Prig" (in Haack 1998: 16 ff.).

14. Stich seems quite close to such a conclusion, for he argues that no norma-
     tive constraints at all weigh upon beliefs (Stich 1990). See below.
15. Davidson (1999), in reply to my claim in Engel (1999a), apparently ac-
     cepts that truth is not a norm, and says that we do not aim at truth, but
     only at "honest justification". His denial is, I have claimed, correct, if he
     wants to oppose the idea that there is some moral obligation to search for
     truth. But I do not see why justification would have to be justification for
     truth, and hence why it cannot be a norm in the sense defended in §4.1
     above. See Engel (2001a).
16. Reprinted in Blackburn & Simmons (1999: 256–7).
17. This is Williams's answer (Williams 1996: 24). Horwich replies (1998b:
     257) that his form of minimalism can handle the notion of an intrinsic
     value if this notion is explained in terms of something "being intrinsically
     conducive to human welfare". But I do not see why this is not begging the
     question.
18. This might seem to be a version of Moore's "open question argument"
     (Moore 1900) but it is not necessarily so. I agree here with Jackson (2000:
     112–13; 1999: 118). His view is a form of cognitivism about norms, but
     of a reductivist kind, although he denies that the reduction can be done in
     the way Horwich proposes. Another option is a form of cognitivism with
     respect to moral properties, but with a claim of nonreductive dependence
     or supervenience.
19. I take it that this is the position of Horwich (1990: 54), who is in no way
     a quietist about philosophical problems in general. He clearly dissociates
     himself from relativism.
20. Davidson's famous argument against conceptual schemes ("On the Very
     Idea of a Conceptual Scheme", in Davidson 1984) is a version of this.
     Some philosophers, however, defend the extreme view that linguistic
     meaning *systematically* underdetermines the truth conditions of a sen-
     tence, that is, that there can never be any stable truth condition for any
     sentence whatsoever (Searle 1978). If they are right, the second argument
     against relativism cannot work But it is unclear how they would respond
     to the others, if their claims can be constructed as arguments in favour of
     relativism.
21. There is a detailed formulation of these arguments in Schmitt (1995: Ch.
     2). For other arguments, see Putnam (1981) and Percival (1994).
22. Lynch characterizes "metaphysical pluralism" as "the idea that there can
     be more than one true metaphysic, that there can be a plurality of *incom-
     patible*, but equally acceptable, conceptual schemes" (1998: 10–11, my
     emphasis) (see also Price 1992). However, Lynch (1998: 151) says: "My
     argument was based in part on the fact that our minimal, basic concept of
     a shared reality is of a world that impinges on all of us. The concept of a
     shared reality is deeply presupposed by our worldview." As Lynch notes,
     this view oscillates, like Goodman's (1978) irrealism, between the idea
     that there as many different words as there are true descriptions or
     "schemes", and the idea that these descriptions are descriptions *of* "the"
     world. But if Lynch's first statement is endorsed, it is not clear that his

metaphysical pluralism is not a form of truth relativism. The perspective underlying MR as it is defended here is closer to a view of metaphysics such as Jackson's (1999) and what he calls "the location problem": where can the various properties of things which are, on the face of it, not natural, find a place within a naturalistic account? Jackson suggests, however, a reductionist strategy in many domains (see above, note 18) I would prefer to suggest a nonreductive, supervenience account.

23. This reasoning is all borrowed from Boghossian's very lucid paper on the Sokal affair (Boghossian 1996).

Conclusion: Truth regained

1. For a similar irreductibilist view, see Williamson (2000: 2–5).
2. The phrase occurs in Frege's criticism of Husserl's early psychologism in his review of his *Philosophie der Arithmetik* (see Frege 1952).
3. Heal (1987) claims this. Haack (1998: 16–18) replies appropriately.
4. On this image of a "bald naturalism", see McDowell (1994: 74).
5. This perspective is also that of "virtue epistemology". See, for instance, Steup (2001), which contains a number of essays furthering the perspective indicated in Chapter 5.
6. See, for instance, Allen (1993) and, for a reaction, Engel (1994b). My claim here should not be taken as an outright rejection of "social epistemology". What I am claiming is that such an epistemology had better not get rid of truth. For such a perspective see in particular Goldman (1999) and, for a more sensible conception of the relationships between knowledge and power than Foucault's, Fricker (1998).

Bibliography

Alexander, S. 1920. *Space, Time and Deity*, The Gifford Lectures 1916–18. London: Macmillan.

Allen, B. 1993. *Truth in Philosophy*. Cambridge, MA: Harvard University Press.

Almeder, R. 1992. *Blind Realism*. New York: Rowman and Littlefield.

Almeder, R. forthcoming. *Real Truth*.

Alston, W. 1996. *A Realist Conception of Truth*. Ithaca, NY: Cornell University Press.

Anscombe, E. 1958. *Intention*. Oxford: Blackwell.

Anselm of Canterbury 1998. *De Veritate*. Translated as *On Truth* in *Anselm of Canterbury, the Major Works*, B. Davies & G. R. Evans (eds). Oxford: Oxford University Press.

Aquinas, T. 1952–4. *Questiones disputatae de veritate*. Translated as *Truth*, R. W. Mulligan, J. V. McGlynn, R. W. Schmidt (trans.). Chicago: Regnery.

Aristotle. *Categories*, Minio Palluelo (ed.). Oxford: Oxford University Press (1949).

Aristotle. *Metaphysics*, W. Jeager (ed.). Oxford: Clarendon Press (1948).

Aristotle. *Metaphysics Gamma*, C. Kirwan (ed.). Oxford: Clarendon Press (1971).

Aristotle. *Nicomachean Ethics*. In *The Complete Works of Aristotle: The Revised Oxford Translation*, J. Barnes (ed.). Princeton, NJ: Princeton University Press (1984).

Armstrong, D. A. 1997. *A World of States of Affairs*. Cambridge: Cambridge University Press.

Armstrong, D. A. 2000. "Difficult Cases in the Theory of Truthmaking", *The Monist* 83(1): 150–60.

Austin, J. L. 1950. "Truth". In *Philosophical Papers*, 117–33. Oxford: Oxford University Press. Reprinted in G. Pitcher (ed.) *Truth*. Englewood Cliffs, NJ: Prentice Hall (1964) and Blackburn & Simmons (1999).

Austin, J. L. 1962. *Sense and Sensibilia*. Oxford: Oxford University Press.

Ayer, A. J. 1936. *Language, Truth and Logic*. London: Gollanz.

Baldwin, T. 1990. *G. E. Moore*. London: Routledge.

Baldwin, T. 1991a. "Can there be a Substantive Account of Truth?" In *New Inquiries into Meaning and Truth*, P. Engel & N. Cooper (eds), 21–39. Hemel Hempstead: Harvester Wheatsheaf.

Baldwin, T. 1991b. "The Identity Theory of Truth", *Mind* 100(5): 45–52.

Barwise, J. & J. Perry 1983. *A Study of Events*. Cambridge: Cambridge University Press.

Benacerraf, P. 1973. "Mathematical Truth", *Journal of Philosophy* 70: 661–80. Reprinted in Benacerraf & Putnam (1983).

Benacerraf, P. & H. Putnam (eds) 1983. *Philosophy of Mathematics, Selected Readings*, 2nd edn. Cambridge: Cambridge University Press.

Bennett, J. 1988. *A Study of Events*. Cambridge: Cambridge University Press.

Bentham, J. 1959. *Bentham's Theory of Fictions*, C. K. Ogden (ed.). London: Routledge.

Blackburn, S. 1985. *Spreading the Word*. Oxford: Oxford University Press.

Blackburn, S. 1990. "Wittgenstein's Irrealism". In *Wittgenstein: eine Neubewehrung*, J. Brandl & R. Haller (eds), 13–26. Vienna: Holder-Richler-Temsky.

Blackburn, S. 1992. *Essays in Quasi-Realism*. Oxford: Oxford University Press.

Blackburn, S. 1998a. *Ruling Passions*. Oxford: Oxford University Press.

Blackburn, S. 1998b. "Wittgenstein, Wright and Minimalism", *Mind* 107(425): 157–81.

Blackburn, S. & K. Simmons (eds) 1999. *Truth*. Oxford: Oxford University Press.

Boghossian, P. 1990. "The Status of Content", *Philosophical Review* 99: 157–84.

Boghossian, P. 1996. "What Sokal's Hoax Ought to Teach Us", *Times Literary Supplement*, 13 December: 14–15.

Bolzano, B. 1837. *Wissenschaftslehre*. Sulbach: Seidel. Translated as *Theory of Science*, Rolf George (ed. and trans.). Oxford: Blackwell, 1972.

Bolzano, B. 1851. *Paradoxien der Unendlichkeit*. Translated as *Paradoxes of the Infinite*, D. A. Steele (trans.). London.

Bradley, F. H. 1914. *Essays on Truth and Reality*. Oxford: Clarendon Press.

Bradley, F. H. 1922. *The Principles of Logic*, 2nd edn. Oxford: Oxford University Press.

Brandom, R. 1994. *Making it Explicit*. Cambridge, MA: Harvard University Press.

Brentano, F. 1930. *Wahrheit und Evidenz*. Leipzig: Meiner. Translated as *The True and the Evident*, R. Chisholm (trans.). London: Routledge (1961).

Burge, T. 1986. "Frege on Truth". In *Frege Synthesised*, J. Hintikka & L. Haaparanta (eds), 97–154. Dordrecht: Reidel.

Candlish, S. 1989. "The Truth about F. Bradley", *Mind* 98: 331–48.

Candlish, S. 1999. "Identifying the Identity Theory of Truth", *Proceedings of The Aristotelian Society* XCIX: 233–40.

Cartwright, N. 1983. *How the Laws of Physics Lie*. Oxford: Oxford University Press.

Child, B. 2000. "Wittgenstein and Common Sense Realism", *Facta* 2(2): 179–202.

Clark, M. 1990. *Nietzsche on Truth and Philosophy*. Cambridge: Cambridge University Press.

Clifford, W. K. 1878. "The Ethics of Belief". In *Lectures and Essays*. New York: Watts, 1947.

Crivelli, P. 1996. "Notes on Aristotle on Truth". In *ΟΔΟΙ ΔΙΖΗΣΙΟΣ, Studi in honore di Franscesco Adorno*, M. Serena Funghi (ed.), 159. Florence: L. S. Olschki.

Crivelli, P. 1999. "Aristotle on the Truth of Utterances", *Oxford Studies in Ancient Philosophy* XVII: 37–56.

Dancy, J. (ed.) 2000. *Normativity*. Oxford: Blackwell.

David, M. 1992. *Correspondence and Disquotation*. Oxford: Oxford University Press.

Davidson, D. 1967. "The Logical Form of Action Sentences". In *Essays on Actions and Events*, D. Davidson. Oxford: Oxford University Press, 1980.

Davidson, D. 1984. *Inquiries into Meaning and Truth*. Oxford: Oxford University Press.

Davidson, D. 1990. "The Structure and Content of Truth", *Journal of Philosophy* 87: 279–328.

Davidson, D. 1995. "The Folly of Trying to Define Truth", *Journal of Philosophy* 93: 263–78. Reprinted in Blackburn & Simmons (1999), 308–50.

Davidson, D. 1999. "Reply to Pascal Engel". In *The Philosophy of Donald Davidson*, L. Hahn (ed.), 460–61. La Salle, IL: Open Court.

de Rijk, L. 1987. "Logos and Pragma in Aristotle". In *Logos and pragma, Festsschrift für Gabriel Nuchelmans*, L. de Rijk (ed.), 27–61. The Hague: Nijhoff.

Deleuze, G. 1962. *Nietzsche et la philosophie*. Paris: PUF. Translated as *Nietzsche and Philosophy*. London: Athlone Press, 1983.

Deleuze, G. 1990. *Pourparlers*. Paris: Minuit.

Derrida, J. 1982. "The White Mythology". In *Margins of Philosophy*, 209–29. Chicago, IL: University of Chicago Press.

Descartes, R. 1964–76. *Œuvres*, C. Adam & P. Tannery (eds). Paris: Vrin. Partial English translation in *The Philosophical Writings of Descartes*, 3 vols, J. Cottingham, R. Stoothoff, D. Murdoch (eds). Cambridge: Cambridge University Press (1985).

Diamond, C. 1996. *The Realist Spirit*. Cambridge, MA: MIT Press.

Dodd, J. 1995. "McDowell and Identity Theories of Truth", *Analysis* 55: 162–5.

Dodd, J. 2001. *The Identity Theory of Truth*. London: Macmillan.

Dokic, J. & P. Engel 2002. *Frank Ramsey, Truth and Success*. London: Routledge.

Dummett, M. 1959. "Truth", *Proceedings of the Aristotelian Society* 59: 141–62. Reprinted in Dummett (1978).

Dummett, M. 1978. *Truth and Other Enigmas*. London: Duckworth.

Dummett, M. 1981. *The Interpretation of Frege's Philosophy*. London: Duckworth.

Dummett, M. 1991. *The Logical Basis of Metaphysic*. Cambridge, MA: Harvard University Press.

Dummett, M. 1996. *The Seas of Language*. Oxford: Oxford University Press.

Elster, J. 1978. *Sour Grapes*. Cambridge: Cambridge University Press.

Engel, P. 1991. *The Norm of Truth: An Introduction to the Philosophy of Logic*. Hemel Hempstead: Harvester Wheatsheaf.

Engel, P. 1994a. *Davidson et la philosophie du langage*. Paris: PUF.

Engel, P. 1994b. "The Decline and Fall of French Nietzscho Structuralism". In *European Philosophy and the American Academy*, B. Smith (ed.), 21–41. La Salle, IL: Open Court.

Engel, P. 1997. *La dispute, une introduction à la philosophie analytique*. Paris: Minuit.

Engel, P. 1998. *La vérité, réflexions sur quelques truismes*. Paris: Hatier.

Engel, P. 1999a. "The Norms of the Mental" In *The Philosophy of Donald Davidson*, L. Hahn (ed.), 447–59. La Salle, IL: Open Court.

Engel, P. 1999b. "Volitionism and Voluntarism about Belief". In *Cognition, Belief and the Will*, A. Meijers (ed.), 9–25. Tilburg: Tilburg University Press.

Engel, P. 1999c. "Analytic Philosophy and Cognitive Norms", *The Monist* 82(2): 218–34.

Engel, P. (ed.) 2000. *Believing and Accepting*. Dordrecht: Kluwer.

Engel, P. 2001a. "Is Truth a Norm?" In *Interpreting Davidson*, P. Pagin & P. Segal (eds), 37–51. Stanford, CA: CSLI.

Engel, P. 2001b. "The False Modesty of the Identity Theory of Truth", *International Journal of Philosophical Studies* 9(4): 441–58.

Engel, P. & N. Cooper (eds) 1991. *New Inquiries into Meaning and Truth*. Hemel Hempstead: Harvester Wheatsheaf.

Feldman, R. 2000. "The Ethics of Belief", *Philosophy and Phenomenological Research* 60(3): 667–95.

Field, H. 1972. "Tarski's Theory of Truth", *Journal of Philosophy* 69: 347–75.

Field, H. 1981. *Science Without Numbers*. Oxford: Blackwell.

Field, H. 1986. "The Deflationary Conception, of Truth". In *Fact, Science and Morality: Essays in Honour of A. J. Ayer*, G. McDonald & C. Wright (eds), 55–117. Oxford: Blackwell.

Field, H. 1993. *Realism, Mathematics and Modality*. Oxford: Oxford University Press.

Field, H. 1994. "Deflationism Views of Meaning and Content", *Mind* 103: 249–84. Reprinted in Blackburn & Simmons (1999), 350–91.

Field, H. 1995. "Deflationism and Factually Defective Discourse", *Philosophical Review* 103(3): 405–52.

Fine A. 1984. "The Natural Ontological Attitude". In *Scientific Realism*, J. Leplin (ed.), 83–107. Berkeley, CA: University of California Press.

Fine A. 1986. *The Shaky Game*. Chicago, IL: Chicago University Press.

Fitch, F. 1963. "A Logical Analysis of some Value Concepts", *Journal of Symbolic Logic* 28: 135–42.

Forbes, G. 1986. "Truth, Correspondence and Redundancy" In *Fact, Science and Morality: Essays in Honour of A. J. Ayer*, G. McDonald & C. Wright (eds), 27–54. Oxford: Blackwell.

Foucault, M. 1997. "On the Genealogy of Ethics". In *Ethics*, M. Foucault, 260–79. Harmondsworth: Penguin.

Frege, G. 1918. *Der Gedanke*, translated as "The Thought". In *Translations from the Philosophical Writings of G. Frege*, P. Geach & A. Kenny (trans.). Oxford: Blackwell, 1952. Reprinted in Strawson (1967), 17–38.

Frege, G. 1952. *Translations from the Philosophical Writings of G. Frege*, P. Geach & A. Kenny (trans.). Oxford: Blackwell.

Frege, G. 1979. *Posthumous Writings*, P. Long & R. White (trans.). Oxford: Blackwell.

Frege, G. 1981. *Philosophical and Mathematical Correspondence*, P. Long & R. White (trans.). Oxford: Blackwell.

Fricker, M. 1998. "Rational Authority and Social Power: Toward a Truly Social Epistemology", *Proceedings of the Aristotelian Society* 98: 159–78.

Geach, P. 1965. "Assertion", *Philosophical Review* 74: 449–65. Reprinted in Geach (1968).

Geach, P. 1968. *Logic Matters*. Oxford: Blackwell.

Gettier, E. 1963. "Is Justified True Belief Knowledge?", *Analysis* 23: 121–3.

Gibbard, A. 1990. *Wise Choices, Apt Feelings*. Cambridge, MA: Harvard University Press.

Gibbard, A. forthcoming. "Explaining with Mental Content".

Gibson, J. J. 1979. *The Ecological Approach to Visual Perception*. Boston, MA: Houghton Mifflin.

Goldman, A. 1999. *Knowledge in a Social World*. Oxford: Oxford University Press.

Goldstein, L. 2000. "Moore's Paradox". In *Believing and Accepting*, P. Engel (ed.), 65–92. Dordrecht: Kluwer.

Goodman, N. 1978. *Ways of Worldmaking*. Indianapolis, IN: Hackett.

Gregory of Rimini 1522. *Commentarium de Primo Libro Sententiarum*. Reprinted by the Franciscan Institute, 1955.

Grover, D. 1992. *A Prosentential Theory of Truth*. Princeton, NJ: Princeton University Press.

Gupta, A. 1993. "A Critique of Deflationism", *Philosophical Topics* 21(2): 57–81. Reprinted in Blackburn & Simmons (1999), 282–307.

Haack, S. 1987. "Surprising Noises", *Proceedings of the Aristotelian Society* 88: 293–302.

Haack, S. 1993. *Evidence and Inquiry*. Oxford: Blackwell.

Haack, S. 1997. "The Ethics of Belief Reconsidered". In *The Philosophy of Roderick Chisholm*, L. Hahn (ed.), 129–44. La Salle, IL: Open Court.

Haack, S. 1998. *Manifesto of a Passionate Moderate*. Chicago, IL: Chicago University Press.

Hacking, I. 1983. *Representing and Intervening*. Cambridge: Cambridge University Press.

Hahn, L. (ed.) 1999. *The Philosophy of Donald Davidson*. La Salle, IL: Open Court.

Haldane, J. 1993. "Mind-World Identity and the Anti-realist Challenge". In *Reality, Representation and Projection*, J. B. Haldane & C. Wright (eds), 1–37. Oxford: Oxford University Press.

Haldane, J. B. & C. Wright (eds) 1993. *Reality, Representation and Projection*. Oxford: Oxford University Press.

Hale, B. 1997. "Realism and its Oppositions". See Hale & Wright (1997), 271–308.

Hale B. & C. Wright (eds) 1997. *A Companion to the Philosophy of Language*. Oxford: Blackwell.

Heal, J. 1987. "The Disinterested Search for Truth". *Proceedings of the Aristotelian Society* 88: 97–108.

Hegel, G. 1975. *Encyclopedia of the Philosophical Sciences*, W. Wallace (trans.). Oxford: Clarendon Press.

Heidegger, M. 1931. *Von Wesen der Wahrheit*. Frankfurt: Klostermann, 1988. Translated in *Pathmarks*, W. McNeill (ed.). Cambridge: Cambridge University Press (1998).

Hesse, M. 1966. *Models and Analogies in Science*. Notre Dame, IN: University of Notre Dame Press.

Hesse, M. 1984. "The Cognitive Claims of Metaphor". In *Metaphor and Religion: Theolinguistics*, vol. 2, J. P. Van Nope (ed.). Brussels.

Hesse, M. 1987. "Reply to Rorty", *Proceeedings of the Aristotelian Society* 61: 297–311.

Hooker, B. (ed.) 1996. *Truth in Ethics*. Oxford: Blackwell.

Hornsby, J. 1998. "Truth, the Identity Theory", *Proceedings of the Aristotelian Society* 97: 1–24.

Horwich, P. 1990. *Truth*. Oxford: Oxford University Press.

Horwich, P. 1996. "Realism Minus Truth", *Philosophy and Phenomenological Research* 56(4): 877–81.

Horwich, P. 1998a. *Meaning*. Oxford: Oxford University Press.

Horwich, P. 1998b. *Truth*, 2nd edn. Oxford: Oxford University Press.

Hume, D. 1748. *A Treatise of Human Nature*, L. A. Selby-Bigge (ed.). Oxford: Clarendon Press (1968).

Husserl, E. 1900–1901. *Logische Untersuchungen*. Halle: Niemeyer. Translated as *Logical Investigations*, J. N. Findlay (trans.). London: Routledge, 1970.

Jackson, F. 1986. *Conditionals*. Oxford: Blackwell.

Jackson, F. 1999. *From Metaphysics to Ethics*. Oxford: Oxford University Press.

Jackson, F. 2000. "Non Cognitivism, Normativity, Belief". In *Normativity*, J. Dancy (ed.), 100–15. Oxford: Blackwell.

Jackson, F, G. Oppy & M. Smith 1994. "Minimalism and Truth Aptness", *Mind* 103: 287–302.

James, W. 1897. "The Will to Believe". In *The Will to Believe and Other Essays*, 1–30. New York: Dover Books.

James, W. 1907. *Pragmatism*. New York: Longmans and Green.

James, W. 1909. *The Meaning of Truth*. London: Longmans and Green.

Joachim, H. 1906. *The Nature of Truth*. Oxford: Clarendon Press.

Johnson, W. E. 1920. *Logic*. Cambridge: Cambridge University Press.

Johnston, M. 1993. "Objectivity Refigured; Pragmatism without Verificationism". In *Reality, Representation and Projection*, J. B. Haldane & C. Wright (eds), 85–132. Oxford: Oxford University Press.

Kant, I. 1781. *Kritik der Reinen Vernunft*. Translated as *Critique of Pure Reason*, N. Kemp Smith (trans.). London: Macmillan (1929).

Kenny, A. & J. Pinborg 1982. *The Cambridge History of Later Medieval Philosophy*. Cambridge: Cambridge University Press.

Kirkham, R. 1992. *Theories of Truth*. Cambridge, MA: MIT Press.

Kraut, R. 1993. "Robust Deflationism", *Philosophical Review* 102: 247–63.

Kripke, S. 1975. "Outline of a Theory of Truth", *Journal of Philosophy* 72: 690–716.

Künne, W. forthcoming. *Conceptions of Truth*. Oxford: Oxford University Press.

Leibniz, G. W. 1705. *Nouveaux Essais sur l'entendement humain*. Translated as *New Essays on Human Understanding*, P. Remnant & J. Bennett (trans.). Cambridge: Cambridge University Press (1981).

Lewis, D. 1986. "Truth in Fiction". In *Philosophical Papers*, vol. 1. Oxford: Oxford University Press.

Lewis, D. 1987. *The Plurality of Worlds*. Oxford: Blackwell.

Lynch, M. 1998. *Truth in Context*. Cambridge, MA: MIT Press.

Lynch, M. (ed.) 2001a. *The Nature of Truth*. Cambridge, MA: MIT Press.

Lynch, M. 2001b. "A Functionalist View of Truth". In *The Nature of Truth*, M. Lynch (ed.). Cambridge, MA: MIT Press.

Mackie, J. 1973. *Truth, Probability and Paradox*. Oxford: Clarendon Press.

Mackie, J. 1977. *Ethics, Inventing Right or Wrong*. Harmondsworth: Penguin.

Maddy, P. 1990. *Realism in Mathematics*. Oxford: Oxford University Press.

Martin, R. 1984. *Recent Essays on Truth and the Liar Paradox*. Oxford: Oxford University Press.

McDowell, J. 1981, "Anti-realism and the Epistemology of Understanding". In *Meaning and Understanding*, J. Bouveresse & H. Parret (eds), 225–48. Berlin: De Gruyter. Reprinted in McDowell (1998).

McDowell, J. 1987. "In Defense of Modesty". In *Dummett: Contributions to Philosophy*, B. Taylor, 59–80. The Hague: Nijoff. Reprinted in McDowell (1998).

McDowell, J. 1994. *Mind and World*. Cambridge, MA: Harvard University Press.

McDowell, J. 1998. *Meaning, Knowledge and Reality*. Cambridge, MA: Harvard University Press.

Mellor, D. H. 1991. *Matters of Metaphysics*. Cambridge: Cambridge University Press.

Millikan, R. 1984. *Language, Thought, and Other Biological Categories*. Cambridge, MA: MIT Press.

Misak, C. 1991. *Truth and the End of Inquiry*. Oxford: Oxford University Press.

Moore, A. W. 1997. *Points of View*. Oxford: Oxford University Press.

Moore, G. E. 1901. "Truth and Falsity". In *Dictionary of Philosophy and Psychology*, J. Baldwin (ed.), 20–22. London: Macmillan. Reprinted in G. E. Moore, *Selected Writings*, T. Baldwin (ed.), 20–22. London: Routledge, 1993.

Moore, G. E. 1903. *Principia Ethica*. Cambridge: Cambridge University Press.

Moore, G. E. 1993. *Philosophical Papers*, T. Baldwin (ed.). London: Routledge.

Moreland, J. P. 2001. *Universals*. Chesham: Acumen.

Mulligan, K., B. Smith & P. Simons 1984. "Truth-makers", *Philosophy and Phenomenological Research* **44**(3): 287–321.

Neale, S. 1995. "The Philosophical Significance of Gödel's Slingshot", *Mind* **104**(416): 761–825.

Neale, S. 2001. *Facing Facts*. Oxford: Oxford University Press.

Nietzsche, F. 1966. *The Gay Science*, W. Kaufmann (trans.). New York: Vintage.

Nietzsche, F. 1979. "On Truth and Lies in the Moral Sense". In *Philosophy and Truth: Selections from Nietzsche's Notebooks in the Early 1870*, D. Brazaele (trans.). Atlantic Highlands, NJ: Humanities Press.

Nietzsche, F. 1988. *Human, All Too Human*, R. J. Hollingdale (trans.). Cambridge: Cambridge University Press.

Noordhof, P. 2001. "Believe What You Want", *Proceedings of the Aristotelian Society* **101**: 247–65.

O'Leary Harwthorne, J. & G. Oppy 1997. "Minimalism and Truth", *Nous* **31**: 170–96.

Owens, D. 2000. *Reason Without Freedom: The Problem of Epistemic Normativity*. London: Routledge.

Papineau, D. 1987. *Reality and Representation*. Oxford: Blackwell.

Peacocke, C. 1992. *A Study of Concepts*. Cambridge. MA: MIT Press.

Peacocke, C. 1993. "Proof and Truth". In *Reality, Representation and Projection*, J. B. Haldane & C. Wright (eds), 165–90. Oxford: Oxford University Press

Peacocke, C. 1999. *Being Known*. Oxford: Oxford University Press.

Peirce, C. S. 1935–1958. *Collected Papers,* 8 vols, A. Burks & P. Weiss (eds). Cambridge, MA: Harvard University Press.

Percival, P. 1994. "Absolute Truth", *Proceedings of the Aristotelian Society* **94**: 189–213.

Perry, R. B. 1935. *The Thought and Character of William James*, 2 vols. Boston: Little, Brown.

Pettit, P. 1996. "Realism and Truth: A Comment on Wright's *Truth and Objectivity*", *Philosophy and Phenomenological Research* **56**(4): 883–90.

Plantinga, A. 1982. "How Not to be Anti-Realist", *Proceedings and Addresses of the American Philosophical Association*, 5647–70.

Plato. *Euthyphro*, H. N. Fowler (trans.), Loeb Classical Library. Cambridge, MA: Harvard University Press (1914).

Popper, K. 1972. *Objective Knowledge*. Oxford: Oxford University Press.

Price, H. 1988. *Facts and the Value of Truth*. Oxford: Blackwell.

Price, H. 1992. "Metaphysical Pluralism", *Journal of Philosophy* **89**(8): 387–409.

Prior, A. 1971. *Objects of Thought*. Oxford: Oxford University Press.

Psillos, S. 1998. *Scientific Realism*. London: Routledge.

Putnam, H. 1971. *Philosophy of Logic*. New York: Harper.

Putnam, H. 1975–83. *Philosophical Papers*, 3 vols. Cambridge: Cambridge University Press.

Putnam, H. 1981. *Reason, Truth and History*. Cambridge: Cambridge University Press.

Putnam, H. 1990. *Realism with a Human Face*. Cambridge, MA: Harvard University Press.

Putnam, H. 1994. "Sense, Non Sense and the Senses: An Inquiry into the Powers of the Human Mind", Dewey Lectures, *Journal of Philosophy* 91: 445–517. Reprinted as *The Threefold Chord*. Chicago: University of Chicago Press, 1999.

Quine, W. V. O. 1960. *Word and Object*. Cambridge, MA: MIT Press.

Quine, W. V. O. 1970. *Philosophy of Logic*. Englewood Cliffs: Prentice Hall.

Quine, W. V. O. 1990. *Pursuit of Truth*. Cambridge, MA: Harvard University Press.

Ramsey, F. P. 1930. "Facts and Propositions". In *The Foundations of Mathematics and Other Essays*, R. Braithwaite (ed.). London: Routledge. Reprinted in Ramsey (1990).

Ramsey, F. P. 1990. *Philosophical Papers*, D. H. Mellor (ed.). Cambridge: Cambridge University Press.

Ramsey, F. P. 1991. *On Truth*, N. Rescher & U. Majer (eds). Dordrecht: Kluwer.

Récanati, F. 2000. "The Simulation of Belief". In *Believing and Accepting*, P. Engel (ed.), 267–98. Dordrecht: Kluwer.

Rescher, N. 1973. *The Coherence Theory of Truth*. Oxford: Clarendon Press.

Resnik, M. 1997. *Mathematics as a Science of Patterns*. Oxford: Oxford University Press.

Rorty, R. 1979. *Philosophy and the Mirror of Nature*. Princeton, NJ: Princeton University Press.

Rorty, R. 1982. *Consequences of Pragmatism*. Hassock: Harvester Press.

Rorty, R. 1986. "Pragmatism, Davidson and Truth". In *Truth and Interpretation*, E. Le Pore (ed.), 323–55. Oxford: Blackwell.

Rorty, R. 1987. "Unfamiliar Noises", *Proceeedings of the Aristotelian Society* 61: 283–96.

Rorty, R. 1991. *Objectivity, Relativism and Truth*. Cambridge: Cambridge University Press.

Rorty, R. 1995. "Is Truth a Goal of Inquiry? Davidson vs Wright", *The Philosophical Quarterly* 45(180): 287–300.

Russell, B. 1911. *The Problems of Philosophy*. London: Home University Library. Reprinted by Oxford University Press, 1968.

Russell, B. 1912. "On the Notion of Cause", *Proceedings of the Aristotelian Society* 13: 1–26. Reprinted in *Mysticism and Logic*, Ch. 10, London: Allen & Unwin (1917).

Russell, B. 1914. "Mysticism and Logic". In *Mysticism and Logic*, B. Russell, 10th impression, 20–48. London: Allen & Unwin (1986).

Russell, B. 1944. *An Inquiry into Meaning and Truth*. London: Allen & Unwin.

Russell, B. 1966. *Philosophical Essays* (1903–1909). London: Allen & Unwin.

Ryle, G. 1950. "'If', 'So' and 'Because'". In *Philosophical Analysis*, M. Black (ed.), 323–40. Ithaca, NY: Cornell University Press. Reprinted in *Collected Papers*, vol. 1. London: Hutchinson, 1971.

Sainsbury, R. M. 1996. "Crispin Wright, *Truth and Objectivity*", *Philosophy and Phenomenological Research* 56(4): 899–904.

Schanz, R. (ed.) 2002. *What is Truth?* Berlin and New York: de Gruyter.

Schmitt, F. 1995. *Truth: A Primer*. Boulder, CO: Westview Press.

Schulz, G. 1993. *Veritas est adaequatio intellectus et rei. Untersuchungen zur Wahrheitslehre des Thomas von Aquin und zur Kritik Kants an einem überlieferten Wahrheitsbegriff*. Leyden: Brill.

Searle, J. 1969. *Speech Acts*. Cambridge: Cambridge University Press.

Searle, J. 1978. "Literal Meaning", *Erkenntnis* 13(1): 207–24. Reprinted in Searle (1979).

Searle, J. 1979. *Expression and Meaning*. Cambridge: Cambridge University Press.

Sellars, W. 1963. *Science, Perception and Reality*. London: Routledge.

Shand, J. 1994. *Philosophy and Philosophers*. London: Penguin Books (2nd edn Chesham: Acumen, 2002).

Shapiro, S. 1998. " Proof and Truth, through Thick and Thin", *Journal of Philosophy* 95: 10.

Simmons, K. 1993. *Universality and the Liar: An Essay on Truth and the Diagonal Argument*. Cambridge: Cambridge University Press.

Skorupski, J. 1997a. "Meaning, Verification and Use". See Hale & Wright (1997), 29–59.

Skorupski, J. 1997b. "Reasons and Reasons". In *Ethics and Practical Reason*, G. Cullity & B. Gaut (eds), 345–67. Oxford: Clarendon Press.

Skorupski, J. 2000. "Irrealist Cognitivism". In *Normativitiy*, J. Dancy (ed.), 116–39. Oxford: Blackwell.

Smith, B. (ed.) 1982. *Parts and Moments*. Munich: Philosophia Verlag.

Smith, B. 1999. "Truthmaker Realism", *Australasian Journal of Philosophy* 77(3): 274–91.

Smith, M. 1994a. "Why Expressivists about Value Should Love Minimalists about Truth", *Analysis* 54: 1–12.

Smith, M. 1994b. *The Moral Problem*. Oxford: Blackwell.

Soames, S. 1984. "What Would be a Theory of Truth?", *Journal of Philosophy* 81(8): 411–29.

Soames, S. 1999. *Understanding Truth*. Oxford: Oxford University Press.

Sosa, E. 1993. "Epistemology, Realism and Truth", *Philosophical Perspectives* 7: 1–7.

Stern, R. 1993. "Did Hegel Hold an Identity Theory of Truth?", *Mind* 102: 645–7.

Steup, M. (ed.) 2001. *Knowledge, Truth and Duty*. Oxford: Oxford University Press.

Stich, S. 1982. *From Folk Psychology to Cognitive Science*. Cambridge, MA: MIT Press.

Stich, S. 1990. *The Fragmentation of Reason*. Cambridge, MA: MIT Press.

Strawson, P. F. 1950. "Truth". In *Logico-Linguistic Papers*, 190–213. London: Methuen.

Strawson, P. F. (ed.) 1967. *Philosophical Logic*. Oxford: Oxford University Press.

Tarski, A. 1930. "The Concept of Truth in Formalised Languages". In *Logic, Semantics, Metamathematics*, A. Tarski & J. Corcoran (eds), 152–278. Indianapolis, IN: Hackett.

Tarski, A. 1944. "The Semantic Theory of Truth" In *Readings in Philosophical Analysis*, H. Feigl & W. Sellars (eds), 52–84. Englewood Cliffs, NJ: Prentice Hall (1949).

Tarski, A. 1983. *Logic, Semantics, Metamathematics*, J. Corcoran (ed.). Indianapolis, IN: Hackett.

Taylor, B. 1976. "States of Affairs". In *Truth and Meaning*, G. Evans & J. McDowell (eds), 264–84. Oxford: Oxford University Press.

Tennant, N. 1987. *Anti-realism and Logic: Truth as Eternal*. Oxford: Oxford University Press.

Tennant, N. 1997. *The Taming of the True*. Oxford: Oxford University Press.

Tiercelin, C. 1998. "Peirce's Objective Idealism: A Defense", *Transactions of the C. S. Peirce Society* 34(1): 1–28.

Unger, P. 1975. *Ignorance*. Oxford: Oxford University Press.

Van Cleve, J. 1996. "Minimal Truth is Realist Truth", *Philosophy and Phenomenological Research* 56(4): 869–75.

Van Fraassen, B. 1981. *The Scientific Image*. Oxford: Oxford University Press.

Vision, G. 1988. *Modern Anti-Realism and Manufactured Truth*. London: Routledge.

Walker, R. C. 1989. *The Coherence Theory of Truth*. Oxford: Oxford University Press.

Walker, R. C. 1997. "Theories of Truth". See Hale & Wright (1997), 309–30.

Whyte, J. 1990. "Success Semantics", *Analysis* 50: 149–57.

Wiggins, D. 1980. "What Would be a Substantial Theory of Truth?" In *Philosophical Subjects, Essays Presented to P. F. Strawson*, Z. Van Staaten (ed.), 189–221. Oxford: Oxford University Press.

Wiggins, D. 1987. *Need, Values, Truth*. Oxford: Blackwell (2nd edn, 1991).

Wiggins, D. 1997. "Meaning and Truth Conditions, From Frege's Grand Design to Davidson". See Hale & Wright (1997), 3–28.

Wiggins, D. forthcoming. "Marks of Truth: An Indefinibilist cum Normative View". In *What is Truth?* R. Schanz (ed.). Berlin and New York: de Gruyter.

Williams, B. 1970. "Deciding to Believe". In *Problems of the Self*, B. Williams, 136–51. Cambridge: Cambridge University Press, 1973.

Williams, B. 1996. "Truth in Ethics". In *Truth in Ethics*, B. Hooker (ed.), 19–34. Oxford: Blackwell.

Williams, C. J. F. 1976. *What is Truth?* Cambridge: Cambridge University Press.

Williams, C. J. F. 1985. *Being, Identity and Truth*. Oxford: Oxford University Press.

Williams, M. 1986. "Do We (Epistemologists) Need a Theory of Truth?", *Philosophical Topics* 14: 223–42.

Williamson, T. 1994a. *Vagueness*. London: Routledge.

Williamson, T. 1994b. "Review of C. Wright, *Truth and Objectivity*", *International Journal of Philosophical Studies* 2: 130–44.

Williamson, T. 1996. "Unreflective Realism", *Philosophy and Phenomenological Research* 56: 905–9.

Williamson, T. 1999. "Truthmakers and the Converse Barcan Formula", *Dialectica* 53(4/5): 253–70.

Williamson, T. 2000. *Knowledge and its Limits*. Oxford: Oxford University Press.

Winters, B. 1979. "Believing at Will", *Journal of Philosophy* 76: 243–56.

Wittgenstein, L. 1921. *Tractatus Logico-Philosophicus* D. Pears & B. McGuinness (trans.), 2nd edn. London: Routledge, 1971.

Wittgenstein, L. 1956. *Remarks on the Foundations of Mathematics*, G. H. Von Wright, R. Rhees & G. E. M. Anscombe (eds). Oxford: Basil Blackwell.

Wittgenstein, L. 1958. *Philosophical Investigations*, 2nd edn. Oxford: Blackwell.

Wittgenstein, L. 1969. *Philosophical Grammar*. Blackwell: Oxford.

Woltersdorff, N. 1996. *Locke and the Ethics of Belief.* Cambridge: Cambridge University Press.

Wright, C. 1983. *Frege's Conception of Numbers as Objects*. Aberdeen: Aberdeen University Press.

Wright, C. 1987. *Realism, Meaning and Truth*. Oxford: Oxford University Press (2nd edn, 1993).

Wright, C. 1988. "What Numbers can Believably Be", *Revue Internationale de philosophie*, 42(167): 425–73.

Wright, C. 1992. *Truth and Objectivity*. Harvard: Harvard University Press.

Wright, C. 1996a. "Replies to Critics", *Philosophy and Phenomenological Research* 56(4): 905.

Wright, C. 1996b. "Truth in Ethics". In *Truth in Ethics*, B. Hooker (ed.). Oxford: Blackwell.

Wright, C. 1998. "Comrades against Quietism", *Mind* 107: 183–283.

Wright, C. 1999. "Truth: A Traditional Debate Reviewed", *Canadian Journal of Philosophy* supp. vol. 24. Reprinted in Blackburn & Simmons (1999), 203–32.

Wright, C. 2000. "Truth as Sort of Epistemic: Putnam's Peregrinations", *Journal of Philosophy* 97(6): 335–64.

Index